Missouri Then and Now
Activity Book

Missouri Then and Now Activity Book

Teacher's Edition

Pamela Fleming Lowe

University of Missouri Press
Columbia and London

Library of Congress Cataloging-in-Publication Data

Lowe, Pamela Fleming, 1961–
  Missouri then and now activity book / Pamela Fleming Lowe.— Teacher's ed.
      p. cm.
ISBN 0-8262-1539-4 (alk. paper)
 1. Missouri—Juvenile literature. 2. Missouri—History—Juvenile literature. 3. Missouri—Study and teaching
(Elementary)—Activity programs. 4. Missouri—History—Study and teaching (Elementary)—Activity programs.
I. Title.
 F466.3.L69 2004
 977.8—dc22

                                                                                    2004008807

Designer: Pamela Fleming Lowe
Printer and binder: Thomson-Shore, Inc.
Typeface: Agency FB

Additional copies of the Teacher's Edition of *"Missouri Then and Now" Activity Book* are available for purchase.

To order, contact the University of Missouri Press,
2910 LeMone Blvd., Columbia, Missouri 65201, or call 1-800-828-1894
and charge your order to a Visa, Discover, or MasterCard account.

All orders are shipped within 48 hours.

Contents

Teachers,

I am pleased to present to you the *"Missouri Then and Now"* Activity Book. A companion for the textbook *Missouri Then and Now* and its Teacher's Guide by Perry McCandless and William E. Foley, it was created with students, teachers, and curriculum designers in mind. The activity book was written from a teacher's perspective to reinforce student knowledge of Missouri's history as well as to provide valid assessments containing cognitive activities, including writing assignments. Teachers will enjoy the rich mixture of traditional lessons and innovative ideas that are in the forefront of learning models today. As a teacher myself, I am very excited about this activity book. It promotes the type of open-ended thinking that is required to challenge students, foster lifelong learners, and to assist students taking the Missouri Assessment Program.

There are several features here that teachers will find helpful in preparing students to learn more about Missouri history and to develop critical thinking skills, as well as to guide them to claim ownership of their education. The activity book offers flexibility in teaching and scoring. Teachers can decide when students may use the textbook as a reference and whether to use the scoring guides in evaluating responses. Scoring guides are provided for daily student writing, diagrams, and projects. These guides may be copied for classroom use. Teachers can choose when and how to use them, as well as how to distribute points. Space is also provided for additional scoring criteria. In addition, special scoring guides are provided for specific questions in the chapter assessments .

Another positive feature of this book is the set of student writing activities that will foster good writing skills. Students will have regular practice in answering in-depth questions by restating the questions and supporting their ideas using good writing form.

This book also allows for student flexibility in that many of the activities allow them to choose the type of format they wish to use to demonstrate knowledge and critical thinking skills. Students will benefit from the streamlined vocabulary activities that focus on direct instruction and non-linguistic representation. We know that students gain knowledge when it is acquired and represented verbally and visually in the memory. By pinpointing specific vocabulary words from the chapters and encountering them in a variety of contexts, students will assimilate new words and terms in a more comprehensive fashion than with traditional definition and flashcard methods.   Students will also benefit from the Objectives pages, which are great for note-taking during class discussions and while reading the textbook chapters. This activity replaces the traditional fill-in-the-blank study-guide activity and encourages students to become proactive in their education.

Curriculum developers and educators alike will appreciate the combination of conventional and modern assessments, which are aligned to the Grade Level Expectations and the Missouri Show-Me Standards. They will value the open-ended constructed-response items that promote thinking skills, and the extension of knowledge offered by the lessons that incorporate web sites to enhance the textbook chapters.

The *"Missouri Then and Now"* Activity Book was created for you and with your students' education in mind. I hope that you both enjoy the trip across our great state through these pages.

Sincerely,
Pamela Fleming Lowe

Writing/Illustration Scoring Guide

This guide can be used to score writing and illustration activities throughout the book. Use the blank version on the back of this page as a template to create as many copies as needed.

Assignment Criteria	Advanced: _____ Points	Proficient: _____ Points	Developing: _____ Points	Attempted: _____ Points	Teacher Comments
Main Idea	Main idea stands out and is supported by detailed information. Student knowledge very apparent.	Main idea is clear but the supporting information is general. Student knowledge appears general.	Main idea is somewhat clear but supporting information is vague.	The main idea is not clear. There is a random collection of information.	
Topic Support	Relevant, quality details give important information that clearly exceeds assignment.	Supporting details and information are pertinent, but one key issue or portion of the topic information is unsupported.	Supporting details and information are applicable, but several key issues or portions of the topic information are unsupported.	Supporting details and information are unclear, not related to the topic, or inaccurately reported.	
Organization	Paragraph has exceptionally well-organized information.	Paragraph has well-organized information.	Paragraph has organized information.	Organization of information is confusing to the reader.	
Grammar, Spelling, & Punctuation	No grammatical, spelling, or punctuation errors.	Almost no grammatical, spelling, or punctuation errors	A few grammatical, spelling, or punctuation errors.	Many grammatical, spelling, or punctuation errors.	
Construction	Paragraph includes introductory sentence, explanations or details, and concluding sentence.	Paragraph includes two of the following: introductory sentence, explanations or details, and concluding sentence.	Paragraph includes related information but is not well constructed.	Paragraph structure is not clear and sentences are not related within the paragraph.	
Illustration	Student identifies ___ important characteristics or ideas.	Student identifies at least ___ important characteristics or ideas.	Student gives ___ characteristics that are distinguishable.	Student has difficulty demonstrating characteristics.	

TOTAL POSSIBLE POINTS : _____   TOTAL GRADE: _____

Writing/Illustration Scoring Guide

Activity: _____   Student's name: _____

Assignment Criteria	Advanced: _____ Points	Proficient: _____ Points	Developing: _____ Points	Attempted: _____ Points	Teacher Comments
Main Idea					
Topic Support					
Organization					
Grammar, Spelling, & Punctuation					
Construction					
Illustration					

TOTAL POSSIBLE POINTS : _____   TOTAL GRADE: _____

Diagram Scoring Guide

This guide can be used to score diagramming activities throughout the book. Use the blank version on the back of this page as a template to create as many copies as needed.

Assignment Criteria	Advanced: _____ Points	Proficient: _____ Points	Developing: _____ Points	Attempted: _____ Points	Teacher Comments
Title of Diagram	Title tells the purpose of the diagram. Title is evident (e.g., large letters, underlined, etc.), and is printed at the top of the diagram.	Title tells the purpose of the diagram and is printed at the top.	Title tells the purpose of the diagram, but is not located at the top.	Purpose of the diagram is not clear from the title.	
Effectiveness of Diagram	90–100% of the labels/features can be read easily.	80–89% of the labels/features can be read easily.	70–79% of the labels/features can be read easily.	Less than 70% of the labels/features can be read easily.	
Organization	The diagram has exceptionally well-organized information.	The diagram has well-organized information.	The diagram has organized information.	The diagram's organization of information is confusing to the reader.	
Similarities/ Differences	At least ___ accurate facts are displayed on the diagram.	___ accurate facts are displayed on the diagram.	___ accurate facts are displayed on the diagram.	Less than ___ accurate facts are displayed on the diagram.	
Content	Covers topic thoroughly with details and examples. Subject knowledge is excellent.	Includes fundamental knowledge about the topic. Subject knowledge appears to be good.	Includes fundamental information about the topic, but there are 1–2 factual errors.	Content is minimal OR there are several factual errors.	

TOTAL POSSIBLE POINTS: _____   TOTAL GRADE: _____

Diagram Scoring Guide

Activity: _____   Student's name: _____

Assignment Criteria	Advanced: _____ Points	Proficient: _____ Points	Developing: _____ Points	Attempted: _____ Points	Teacher Comments
Title of Diagram					
Effectiveness of Diagram					
Organization					
Similarities/ Differences					
Content					

TOTAL POSSIBLE POINTS: _____   TOTAL GRADE: _____

Brochure Scoring Guide

This guide can be used to score the brochure activity in Chapter 17. Use the blank version on the back of this page as a template to create as many copies as needed.

Assignment Criteria	Advanced: _____ Points	Proficient: _____ Points	Developing: _____ Points	Attempted: _____ Points	Teacher Comments
Organization	Each section is easily distinguished and has a clear beginning, middle, and end.	Almost all sections of have a clear beginning, middle, and end.	Most sections have a clear beginning, middle, and end.	Less than half of the sections have a clear beginning, middle, and end.	
Accuracy	All facts about the topic are accurate.	90% of the facts are accurate.	Most of the facts are accurate.	More than half of the facts are inaccurate.	
Attractiveness	Exceptionally attractive design and well-organized information.	Attractive design and well-organized information.	Well-organized information.	Design and organization of material are confusing.	
Punctuation	Capitalization and punctuation are correct throughout.	There are 1–2 capitalization and/or punctuation errors.	There are 3-4 capitalization and/or punctuation errors.	There are several capitalization or punctuation errors.	
Illustrations/Graphics	Illustrations or graphics go well with the text and there is a good mix of text and graphics.	Illustrations or graphics go well with the text, but the layout is too busy and distracting.	Illustrations or graphics are present, but there are too few.	Illustrations or graphics do not go with the text.	

TOTAL POSSIBLE POINTS: _____   TOTAL GRADE: _____

Brochure Scoring Guide

Activity: _____   Student's name: _____

Assignment Criteria	Advanced: ____ Points	Proficient: ____ Points	Developing: ____ Points	Attempted: ____ Points	Teacher Comments
Organization					
Accuracy					
Attractiveness					
Punctuation					
Illustrations/Graphics					

TOTAL POSSIBLE POINTS: _____   TOTAL GRADE: _____

MISSOURI HISTORY TRADING CARDS

Create trading cards about important figures from a chapter that will be chosen by your teacher. Write the figures' names and draw their pictures on the front of the cards. Write down information about each person on the back of the cards.

Your students have these cards in their activity books. Have them do this activity with a chapter of your choosing.

MISSOURI HISTORY TRADING CARDS (cont.)

Complete your Missouri history trading cards by writing important information about each person on the back of the cards. Include vital information such as the person's birthplace and years of birth and death as well as the person's contribution to Missouri history.

Missouri Then and Now
Activity Book

CURRICULUM ALIGNMENT	
THE SHOW-ME STANDARDS:	KNOWLEDGE STANDARDS: SS2, SS6
	PROCESS STANDARDS: G1.8
GRADE LEVEL EXPECTATIONS:	SS5, CONCEPT D4, G7
	SS7, CONCEPT A1

VOCABULARY INSIGHTS

1. archaeologist

    a.   Definition: one who studies the people and customs of ancient times from artifacts

    b.   Write a sentence from the chapter using the word:
        Page 2: What we know about them (early Indians) comes from **archaeologists**.
                 Archaeologists are scientists.
                 Sometimes **archaeologists** find spear points, arrowheads, pieces of pottery, tools, and even toys.
        Page 4: What do **archaeologists** know about the first people who came to Missouri?
                 Archaeologists have found the bones of several very large animals that do not live on the earth today.
                 When **archaeologists** dig up these old animal bones, they sometimes find Indian spear points nearby.
        Page 5: **Archaeologists** have found the bones of some of these prehistoric animals in Missouri.
                 Archaeologists also found some spear points among the prehistoric bones.

    c.   Create your own sentence: answers will vary

    d.   Illustrate the word: Answers will vary. Illustrations may or may not be drawings of what the words look like. Some of the words represent ideas rather than things. The illustrations should represent what the words mean in the chapter and to the student. This cognitive activity helps students to recall and relay the meaning of the vocabulary words.

2. bison

    a.   Definition: an animal with a large shaggy head, strong front legs, and short curved horns

    b.   Write a sentence from the chapter using the word:
        Page 4: Early hunters killed huge **bison** with stone-tipped spears.
                 Another huge animal was the prehistoric **bison**.

    c.   Create your own sentence: answers will vary

    d.   Illustrate the word: answers will vary

3. bog

    a.   Definition: soft, wet ground

    b.   Write a sentence from the chapter using the word:
        Page 5:   Sometimes the Native Americans would chase them into a marshy **bog**.

    c.   Create your own sentence: answers will vary

    d.   Illustrate the word: answers will vary

4. game

    a.   Definition: wild animals including birds and fish that are hunted or caught for food and sport

    b.   Write a sentence from the chapter using the word:
        Page 4:   They may have been searching for wild **game**.
                The early hunters who moved into the Americas from Siberia hunted large **game** animals.
        Page 5:   Stone-tipped spears were one of the few weapons early people had for killing large **game**.
        Page 7:   For thousands of years the early hunters lived by killing large **game** animals.
                That changed when there were no more of the big **game** animals left on earth.
                Many think that the big **game** animals had trouble living in the warmer climate.
                After the big **game** animals were gone, the spear-throwing Native Americans had to kill smaller animals
                    for their food.
                They believe the Indians used the nets to trap small **game** animals.

    c.   Create your own sentence: answers will vary

    d.   Illustrate the word: answers will vary

CURRICULUM ALIGNMENT	
THE SHOW-ME STANDARDS:	KNOWLEDGE STANDARDS: SS2, SS5, SS6
	PROCESS STANDARDS: G1.2, 1.6, 1.8, 1.10, 3.5
GRADE LEVEL EXPECTATIONS:	SS2, CONCEPT A1
	SS6, CONCEPT B2

THE EUROPEAN INFLUENCE

The European influx into Missouri changed the lives of Native Americans. The Europeans brought with them many new things that they traded. These items made the lives of the Native Americans much easier.

Using inference skills, describe how trade with the Europeans influenced Native Americans' clothing, meals, travel, and hunting practices. Answers will vary. Some possible answers are below.

Clothing	The Europeans manufactured fabrics and wore continental-styled clothing. When the Native Americans traded for their clothing it changed the way they dressed from their culturally traditional clothing to a more "civilized" clothing.
Meals	Europeans ate different foods and cooked their foods differently. They used different spices as well, to season their food. The Native Americans tried these foods and probably grew to like them. The Europeans brought cattle, which introduced a new meat to the Native Americans. They also grew gardens and introduced new vegetables to the Native Americans.
Travel	The Europeans brought horses, which the Osage Indians called "mystery dogs." The horses made hunting and traveling a little easier for the Native Americans. Europeans also used oxen and wagons.
Hunting Practices	The Native Americans traded for guns and horses that made hunting easier. Many of them could ride and shoot quite well. Eventually, the Europeans wanted Native Americans to give up hunting and become farmers. The settlers cut down forests to build farms, and there were fewer wild animals to hunt. This made the Native Americans unhappy, and some made war with the settlers.

CURRICULUM ALIGNMENT
THE SHOW-ME STANDARDS: KNOWLEDGE STANDARDS: SS2, SS5, SS6
                          PROCESS STANDARDS: G1.2, 1.6, 1.8, 1.10, 2.1, 3.5
GRADE LEVEL EXPECTATIONS: SS2, CONCEPT A1
                          SS7 CONCEPT B2

TIMELINE

Choose five events from Chapter 1 in your textbook and create a timeline. Write an appropriate title for your timeline in the box provided.

Answers will vary. Teachers may choose to use the Diagram Scoring Guide to score the timeline.

MISSOURI
Then and Now
CHAPTER 1: THE FIRST MISSOURIANS

CURRICULUM ALIGNMENT

THE SHOW-ME STANDARDS: KNOWLEDGE STANDARDS: SS2, SS5, SS6
                         PROCESS STANDARDS: G1.2, 1.6, 1.8, 1.10, 3.5
GRADE LEVEL EXPECTATIONS: SS5, CONCEPT D4
                          SS6, CONCEPT B2

IDENTIFYING GROUPS

List five groups of First Missourians, using Chapter 1 in your textbook. Add some details about them in the spaces provided, using complete sentences.

Answers will vary and could include any of the information below:

1.   The Early Hunters

The early hunters hunted large animals, such as mastodons, mammoths, and bison. They hunted using spears made with stone tips. The hunters would sometimes catch the animals by chasing them into bogs where they would become stuck and could be killed. The big animals became extinct and the early hunters had to begin hunting small animals for food. They also gathered berries, plants, and nuts. Many of the early hunters lived in caves for shelter and protection. They sewed clothing using needles made from bone. They used nets and bags to trap small animals and to collect seeds and nuts.

2.   The Woodland Indians

The Woodland Indians, also called the Hopewell people, were mound builders. They were the first Missourians to keep their settlements in the same place for a long time. They were also Missouri's first farmers, and they traded some of their corn to Indians for copper and seashells. They made clay pipes and bowls and began using bows and arrows instead of spears.

3.   The Mississippi People

This group came up the Mississippi from the south and lived along the rivers in the Mississippi Valley. They lived in well-planned cities and towns and surrounded their towns with fences. The largest of their settlements was at Cahokia, Illinois. They were also mound builders and excellent farmers. They stored food and water in clay bottles and jars that they made. They also wove cloth for clothing. When the first explorers from Europe arrived in Missouri, these town dwellers were gone.

4.   The Osage Indians

The Osage Indians were the largest, most powerful Indian group in Missouri. They were hunters and warriors and were big and strong. The men shaved their heads and painted their faces. The Osage were excellent riders because they had horses before the French came to Missouri. The Osage went on three hunting trips each year. The women planted and harvested the crops and prepared the animals killed by the men. The women also built the lodges called long houses and put up and took down the wigwams during hunting trips.

5.   The Missouri Indians
Answers could include any of the groups below.

The Missouri Indians lived much like the Osage Indians. They hunted, farmed, and gathered wild nuts and berries. Their main village was located on the Missouri River in Saline County, where Van Meter State Park is today. They were in Missouri when the French arrived.

The Shawnee, Delaware, Kickapoo, and Peoria Indians moved into Missouri from the east. White men had taken their lands. They came to Missouri to find a place to live. The Sac, Fox, Kansas, and Ioway Indians also hunted and lived in Missouri.

The Indian people got along well with the French settlers but did not get along well with the later American settlers who wanted to take their land and cut the forests to build farms. Soon most of the Indian tribes had to leave Missouri. They headed west where there were fewer settlers.

5

CURRICULUM ALIGNMENT
THE SHOW-ME STANDARDS: KNOWLEDGE STANDARDS: SS2, SS5, SS6
PROCESS STANDARDS: G1.2, 1.6, 1.8, 1.10, 3.5
GRADE LEVEL EXPECTANCIES: SS2, CONCEPT A1; SS4, CONCEPT B2;
SS6, CONCEPT B2; SS7, CONCEPT A1

CAUSE AND EFFECT

The Europeans brought trade to Missouri. Trade and the use of guns changed the Native Americans' lives and environment.
Fill in the cause-and-effect chart detailing the effects on the Native Americans.

THE CAUSE

The European traders arrived in Missouri.

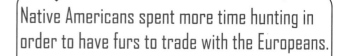

Native Americans spent more time hunting in order to have furs to trade with the Europeans.

There were fewer animals because they killed all the animals they could find.

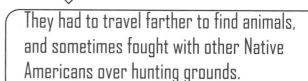

They had to travel farther to find animals, and sometimes fought with other Native Americans over hunting grounds.

Their way of life began to change. They sold most of their animal skins and began using blankets.

MISSOURI
Then and Now
CHAPTER 1: THE FIRST MISSOURIANS

CURRICULUM ALIGNMENT	
THE SHOW-ME STANDARDS:	KNOWLEDGE STANDARDS: SS2, SS5, SS6
	PROCESS STANDARDS: G1.2, 1.6, 1.8, 1.10, 3.5
GRADE LEVEL EXPECTATIONS:	SS2, CONCEPT A1; SS5, CONCEPT D4
	SS6, CONCEPT B2; SS7, CONCEPT B2

CHAPTER 1 ASSESSMENT

Short Answers

1. Who were the first Missourians? the American Indians

2. What type of scientists dig up the ground where early people once lived and look for things that they made? archaeologists

3. Who were Missouri's first real farmers? the Hopewell people

4. What was the worst problem the Indians faced when the Europeans arrived? the diseases the Europeans brought with them

Answer in Two or Three Sentences

5. Explain how Missouri got its name. The word *Missouri* is an Indian word that means "the people who have big canoes." The early French settlers found people living along the great river that flowed into the Mississippi River from the west, and called them the Missouri Indians. The French would put the word *Missouri* on their maps to mark the place where the Missouri Indians lived. They began to call the river the Missouri. Later the U.S. Congress chose the name for our state.

6. Explain in your own words what the Native Americans have given us. The Native Americans have given us many things, including some foods that we eat, such as; corn, potatoes, squash, pumpkins, beans, tomatoes, hominy, succotash, and corn bread. The Indians also gave us canoes, hammocks, pipes, moccasins, buckskin shirts with fringe and parkas. Some Native American words that we use are tomahawk, papoose, hominy, and wigwam. Some Missouri places have Indian names, such as Kansas City, Neosho, Osceola, Miami, and Wyaconda.   The Missouri, Mississippi, Osage, Niangua, and Meramec Rivers have Indian names.

7. How do archaeologists learn things about people that lived long ago? Archaeologists dig up the ground in places where early people once lived. They study the artifacts and bones they find.

8. How do some scientists speculate that Native Americans came to America? They believe that early people from Siberia, searching for wild game, walked across a land bridge that once connected Asia and North America. This strip of land is now covered by the Bering Sea and is called the Bering Strait.

9. What valuable lesson do you think Native Americans learned too late about hunting animals?
The Native Americans killed all the animals they could find in order to trade furs and skins with the Europeans. Eventually the wild-animal population was too low and they had to travel and even fight other Native Americans over hunting grounds. The Native Americans probably learned that they shouldn't kill all of the wild animals in their region in order to have food and clothing for their families.

CHAPTER 1 ASSESSMENT (cont.)

Demonstrating Your Knowledge

10. Write a short paragraph explaining the positive and negative influences the Europeans had on the Native American way of life.
    Answers will vary. Teachers may use the Writing Scoring Guide.

    ### Main Points
    Positive influences: trading of guns, metal knives and kettles, beads, tools, cloth, axes, horses, and jewelry by the Europeans for the Indians' gold jewelry, food, furs, and skins. Negative influences: European diseases, with no cures or vaccinations available to protect the Indians. Students should explain the cultural change for the Native Americans brought about by the civilized products of the Europeans. These products were both a positive and negative influence: positive in that they made the Indians' lives easier and more convenient, and negative in that the Native American customs and way of life was changed forever.

11. Write a short paragraph explaining the importance of the Osage women to their tribe.
    Answers will vary. Teachers may use the Writing Scoring Guide.

    ### Main Points
    The Osage women were the farmers of the tribe. They prepared the field and planted and harvested the crops. At harvest time, they cooked and dried the vegetables. During hunting trips the women prepared the animals killed by the men. They removed the skins and cleaned and tanned them. They cut up the meat and placed it on racks high above the ground to dry. The women later made clothing from the skins. The Osage women also built lodges, or long houses, and during hunting trips they put up and took down the wigwams as the tribe moved from place to place.

CHAPTER 1 ASSESSMENT (cont.)

12. Compare and contrast two Missouri tribes of your choice using a diagram. Include three facts about each tribe and three ways in which the tribes are different. Create a title for your diagram.

    Answers will vary. Teachers may use the Diagram Scoring Guide.

    Students may create a Venn diagram or a chart of some kind. Students may mention the following tribes in their diagrams and at least three of their characteristics:

    Early Hunters
    Moved into the Americas from Siberia.
    Hunted animals including mastodons, bison, and mammoths.
    Used spear points to kill game.
    Made animals run into bogs where they could be killed with spears.
    Began hunting small animals when there were no large animals left on the Earth.
    Lived in caves for protection and shelter.
    Made clothing with skins and needles made of bone.
    Used handmade nets and bags to trap animals and for collecting and storing seeds and nuts.

    Woodland Indians
    Made and used pottery and clay dishes.
    Mound builders.
    The first Missourians to keep their settlements in the same place for a long time.
    Missouri's first real farmers.
    Began to use bows and arrows.
    Traded with other Native Americans.

    Missouri Indians
    Main village was on the Missouri River in Saline County, where Van Meter State Park is located today.
    Lived much like the Osage Indians.
    Hunted, farmed, and gathered wild nuts and berries.
    Some of them did not like white settlers, who cut down the forests to build farms.
    Angry Native Americans and white settlers sometimes attacked each other's homes and made war.
    Most of the tribes had to leave Missouri and move west where there were fewer settlers.

CHAPTER 1 ASSESSMENT (cont.)

(question 12 continued)

Mississippi People (Town Dwellers)
Lived along the rivers in the Mississippi Valley.
Lived in well-planned cities and towns instead of small villages.
Surrounded their cities with high fences.
Largest settlement was at Cahokia, Illinois.
Mound builders.
Many of their cities had a central plaza.
They were excellent farmers and raised enough food to feed the people in their cities.
Made and used clay bottles, pottery, and jars.
Traded with other Native Americans.
Wove cloth.
Disappeared, and no one knows why.

Osage Indians
Largest and most powerful Indian group in Missouri.
The men shaved their heads and painted their faces.
Big and strong.
Already using horses when the French came to Missouri.
Excellent riders and hunters.
The men went on three yearly hunting trips.
The women were the farmers and prepared food.
The women prepared the animals that the men killed.
The women built the lodges and wigwams.
For entertainment they played games, danced, and sang, and the men and boys demonstrated their riding and hunting skills.

Vocabulary
13. Below is a word used in the chapter. In the spaces provided, write a definition of the word, list a synonym for the word, and draw a picture that illustrates the word's meaning.

archaeologist

Definition: one who studies the people and customs of ancient times from artifacts
Synonym: some possible answers are *scientist, paleontologist, anthropologist*
Illustration: answers will vary

14. Explain how the word relates to the chapter. Answers will vary.

CURRICULUM ALIGNMENT		
THE SHOW-ME STANDARDS:	KNOWLEDGE STANDARDS:	SS2, SS6
	PROCESS STANDARDS:	G1.8
GRADE LEVEL EXPECTATIONS:	SS5, CONCEPT D4, G7	
	SS7, CONCEPT A1	

VOCABULARY INSIGHTS

1. continent

    a. Definition: one of the seven great land masses of the earth

    b. Write a sentence from the chapter using the word:
       Page 27: Missouri is located near the center of the North American **continent**.
            Continents are very large land masses.
            The earth has seven **continents**: North America, South America, Africa, Europe, Asia, Australia, and
               Antarctica.
       Page 28: Find each of the **continents** on the map on this page.
       Page 30: Now that you have located the North American **continent**, look at the bodies of water that surround it.

    c. Create your own sentence: answers will vary

    d. Illustrate the word: answers will vary

2. electricity

    a. Definition: a form of energy that can produce light, heat, and motion

    b. Write a sentence from the chapter using the word:
       Page 37: Missourians use their rivers for fishing, boating, swimming, and making **electricity**.
            As the water rushes swiftly through the dam, special turbines in the dam produce **electricity**.

    c. Create your own sentence: answers will vary

    d. Illustrate the word: answers will vary

3. spring

    a.   Definition: a flow of water coming from the earth

    b.   Write a sentence from the chapter using the word:
       Page 33: Big Spring is the largest single **spring** in the United States.
       Page 34: Thousands of **springs** bubble up from the underground water in the Ozarks.
               Big Spring near Van Buren is the largest single **spring** in the United States.

    c.   Create your own sentence: answers will vary

    d.   Illustrate the word: answers will vary

4. soybeans

    a.   Definition: a plant grown for animal food, vegetable oil, flour, and meal

    b.   Write a sentence from the chapter using the word:
       Page 31: Among them are corn, wheat, **soybeans**, tobacco, fruits, and vegetables.

    c.   Create your own sentence: answers will vary

    d.   Illustrate the word: answers will vary

MISSOURI
Then and Now
CHAPTER 2: A RICH LAND

MISSOURI'S FOUR REGIONS

1. Which state is directly south of Missouri? Arkansas

2. Which region contains Blue Springs? Western Plains

3. Starting in Hannibal and traveling south to Rolla, which regions would you pass through? Northern Plains, Ozark Highland

4. Which region is the smallest? Southeast Lowland

5. In which region is the city of Liberty? Northern Plains

6. According to the map, how many regions are in Missouri? four

13

CURRICULUM ALIGNMENT
THE SHOW-ME STANDARDS: KNOWLEDGE STANDARDS: SS2, SS5, SS6, SS7
                          PROCESS STANDARDS: G1.8, 1.10, 3.5, 4.1
GRADE LEVEL EXPECTATIONS: SS5, CONCEPT A1, G7
                           SS7, CONCEPT A1

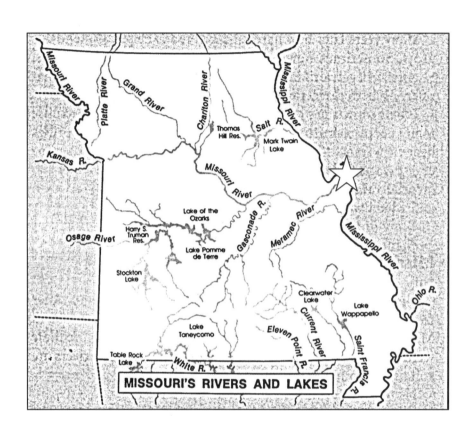

MISSOURI'S RIVERS AND LAKES

1. The Missouri and Mississippi Rivers join near St. Louis. Put a star on the map where the two rivers join.

2. The Mississippi River forms the eastern border of the state of Missouri and flows from the <u>north</u> to the <u>south,</u> down to the Gulf of Mexico.

3. After it flows south down the northwest border of Missouri, the Missouri River generally flows from <u>west</u> to <u>east</u> across the state.

4. The largest lake in the state is the Lake of the Ozarks. If you were to travel west, what river would take you into the state of Kansas? Osage River

5. *Using critical thinking:* List two reasons the chosen location for St. Louis was near two major rivers. Answers will vary. Two possible answers are below.

    a. River travel was excellent for receiving and sending goods and supplies.

    b. Rivers were the quickest way to travel from place to place. They were Missouri's first highways.

CURRICULUM ALIGNMENT

THE SHOW-ME STANDARDS: KNOWLEDGE STANDARDS: SS2, SS5, SS6, SS7
                          PROCESS STANDARDS: G1.8, 1.10, 3.5, 4.1
GRADE LEVEL EXPECTATIONS: SS5, CONCEPT A1, F6
                          SS7, CONCEPT A1

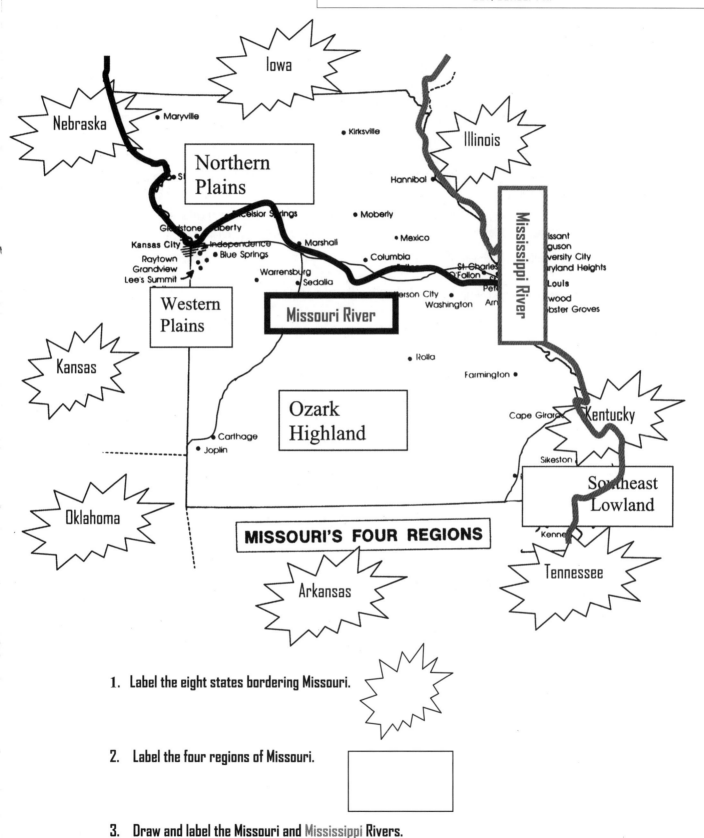

Iowa

Nebraska

• Maryville

• Kirksville

Illinois

Northern
Plains

Hannibal

• Moberly

Excelsior Springs

• Mexico

Gladstone Liberty

Kansas City Independence • Marshall

• Blue Springs

Raytown

Grandview

Lee's Summit

St. Charles

O'Fallon

• Columbia

Warrensburg

Jefferson City

Washington

• Sedalia

Western
Plains

Missouri River

Mississippi River

Kirkwood

Webster Groves

Kansas

• Rolla

Farmington •

Ozark
Highland

Cape Girardeau Kentucky

• Carthage

• Joplin

Sikeston

Southeast
Lowland

Oklahoma

MISSOURI'S FOUR REGIONS

Kennett

Tennessee

Arkansas

1. Label the eight states bordering Missouri.

2. Label the four regions of Missouri.

3. Draw and label the Missouri and Mississippi Rivers.

CURRICULUM ALIGNMENT
THE SHOW-ME STANDARDS: KNOWLEDGE STANDARDS: SS2, SS5, SS6, SS7
                          PROCESS STANDARDS: G1.8, 1.10, 3.5, 4.1
GRADE LEVEL EXPECTATIONS: SS5, CONCEPT D4
                           SS7, CONCEPT A1

TAUM SAUK MOUNTAIN SCAVENGER HUNT

Go to the Taum Sauk Mountain State Park web site to find the answers to the following questions.

http://www.mostateparks.com/taumsauk/geninfo.htm

1. How was Taum Sauk Mountain formed? The history of Taum Sauk Mountain State Park and the St. Francois Mountains began almost 1.5 billion years ago. They were formed by volcanic eruptions that spewed dust, ash, and hot gases. Over the years erosion left only the roots of the mountains behind. Shallow seas periodically covered the remaining knobs, depositing almost a mile of sedimentary dolomite and sandstone on top of the volcanic rhyolite. Uplift of the entire Ozark region and subsequent increased erosion wore away much of the sedimentary rock, once again exposing the ancient rock beneath it.

2. How tall is the mountain at its peak, which is the highest point in Missouri? 1,772 feet above sea level

3. How many acres are in the surrounding park? 7,448

4. In which Missouri region does the mountain reside? the Ozark Highland

5. What is the name for the rocky openings in which you can see the park's volcanic origin? glades

6. What two valuable services do the natural communities of Taum Sauk provide?

    a. They provide relatively undisturbed native habitats for wildlife.

    b. They offer excellent opportunities for scientific research.

7. What is the name of the state's tallest waterfall? Mina Sauk Falls

8. What do the land managers do to help preserve the open woodlands? They use carefully planned prescribed burns.

9. What is the Devil's Tollgate? An eight-foot-wide passage that takes visitors through 50 feet of volcanic rhyolite standing 30 feet high.

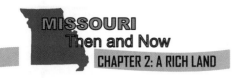

CURRICULUM ALIGNMENT
THE SHOW-ME STANDARDS: KNOWLEDGE STANDARDS: SS2, SS5, SS6
PROCESS STANDARDS: G1.8, 1.10, 3.5, 4.1
GRADE LEVEL EXPECTATIONS: SS5, CONCEPT B2, D4, F6

CHAPTER 2 ASSESSMENT

Vocabulary

1. Below is a word used in the chapter. In the spaces provided, write a definition of the word, list a synonym for the word, and draw a picture that illustrates the word's meaning.

continent

Definition: one of the seven great land masses of the earth

Synonym: some possible answers are *land mass, mainland, land*

Illustration: answers will vary

2. Explain how the word relates to the chapter. Answers will vary.

Short Answers

3. Name the seven continents: Africa, Antarctica, Asia, Australia, Europe, North America, South America

4. On which continent is Missouri located? North America

5. What country is north of the United States? Canada

6. What country is south of the United States? Mexico

7. List the eight states that border Missouri: Iowa, Illinois, Kentucky, Tennessee, Arkansas, Oklahoma, Kansas, Nebraska

8. Name Missouri's two most important rivers: Missouri River, Mississippi River

9. What is the highest point in the state? Taum Sauk Mountain

10. What is Missouri's largest lake? Lake of the Ozarks

11. What type of climate does Missouri have? temperate or cool temperate

17

CHAPTER 2 ASSESSMENT (cont.)

True or False

12. __F__   Missouri is located on the continent of South America.

13. __T__   Canada is located north of the United States.

14. __F__   Mt. Everest is the highest point in Missouri.

15. __T__   The largest lake in Missouri is the Lake of the Ozarks.

16. __T__   The Missouri River and the Mississippi River are Missouri's most important rivers.

17. __F__   Missouri has a polar climate.

18. __F__   The Ozark Highland is the best region for growing crops.

19. __F__   Iowa is south of Missouri.

20. __T__   The Northern Plains has fewer mineral resources than other parts of the state.

Short Answers

21. Why is Missouri sometimes called the "heart of America"?   It is located near the center of the United States.

22. Why did fewer people settle in the Ozarks region of Missouri?   The Ozark Mountains were difficult to travel through and the land was not good for growing crops.

23. Why did so many different Indian peoples decide to live in Missouri?   It has rich soil, valuable minerals, good rivers, plenty of water, and many different plants and animals. Indians came to hunt wild animals, gather food, plant crops, make salt, and mine lead.

CHAPTER 2 ASSESSMENT (cont.)

Demonstrating Your Knowledge

24. Give reasons why early settlers would settle in each of the four Missouri regions.
Answers will vary. Some facts about each region are listed below.

<u>Southeast Lowland:</u> There were several rivers for travel and for water supply. The soil was rich with minerals that were great for farming and growing crops. Since the land is flat and water could not run off easily after the rains, much of this region was swampland for many years. Canals were built to drain the land and make it dry enough for planting crops,

<u>Ozark Highland:</u> Though this region did not contain the best farmland for crops, it had many characteristics that drew settlers. Many settlers came to this region to mine lead. They were also drawn to the many other mineral resources, such as zinc, iron, sand, clay, limestone, and gravel. The region's many forests provided lumber for building homesteads. The area was rich in black walnuts, which is the state nut tree. Settlers also appreciated the many springs that bubbled up from under the ground to provide water.

<u>Western Plains:</u> Settlers may have come to this region to mine coal, which was the most important mineral of the region at one time. Limestone, sand, and gravel were also found here. With its rolling land, this region enabled settlers to grow grain and raise cattle.

<u>Northern Plains:</u> Many settlers came to this region because they found the soil to be good for growing crops. It was also a good place for the livestock business. Finally, many settlers came to this region because it contained many of the largest cities in the state.

CHAPTER 2 ASSESSMENT (cont.)

25. The environment and way of life in Missouri has changed in so many ways since the Native Americans discovered that it was a rich land. Write a paragraph and create an illustration to compare and contrast the Missouri of long ago and the Missouri of today.

    Answers and illustrations will vary. Teachers may use the Writing Scoring Guide at the back of this book.

    Following are some possible answers; students may provide other acceptable answers.

    - The hills and rivers have remained.

    - Some forests remain but many have been cut down for farming and to make room for cities.

    - There are factories now where Indians once lived.

    - Cattle have replaced buffalo grazing.

    - Farming still exists but farmers now use tractors and farming equipment where the Indian women used hoes.

    - The Native American villages are gone, and in their place are cities with skyscrapers.

    - The Indians used canoes to travel downriver; now the rivers carry barges loaded with products.

    - There are more lakes now than when the Indians first discovered Missouri; this is due to the dams built across rivers.

CURRICULUM ALIGNMENT
THE SHOW-ME STANDARDS: KNOWLEDGE STANDARDS: SS2, SS6
                         PROCESS STANDARDS: G1.8
GRADE LEVEL EXPECTATIONS: SS5, CONCEPT D4, G7
                          SS7, CONCEPT A1

VOCABULARY INSIGHTS

1. canoe

    a. Definition: a small light boat moved by paddles

    b. Write a sentence from the chapter using the word:
        Page 51:   The French explorers paddled down the great river in two birchbark **canoes** in 1673.
        Page 52:   La Salle **canoed** all of the way down the Mississippi River to the place where it reached the Gulf of Mexico.

    c. Create your own sentence: answers will vary

    d. Illustrate the word: answers will vary

2. island

    a. Definition: an area of land that is smaller than a continent and completely surrounded by water

    b. Write a sentence from the chapter using the word:
        Page: 49: He had seen a small **island.**

    c. Create your own sentence: answers will vary

    d. Illustrate the word: answers will vary

VOCABULARY INSIGHTS (cont.)

3. kettle

    a. Definition: a pot used for boiling liquids

    b. Write a sentence from the chapter using the word:
        Page 55: Indians came to Fort Orleans to trade their furs for such things as blankets, cloth, mirrors, combs, needles, thimbles, axes, knives, iron **kettles**, and guns.

    c. Create your own sentence: answers will vary

    d. Illustrate the word: answers will vary

4. perfumes

    a. Definition: liquids with the sweet smell of flowers

    b.   Write a sentence from the chapter using the word:
        Page 47: Europeans also liked the **perfumes**, fine silks, beautiful carpets, and precious stones that came from the Orient.

    c. Create your own sentence: answers will vary

    d. Illustrate the word: answers will vary

MISSOURI Then and Now
CHAPTER 3: EUROPE DISCOVERS . . .

CURRICULUM ALIGNMENT	
THE SHOW-ME STANDARDS:	KNOWLEDGE STANDARDS: SS2, SS5, SS6
	PROCESS STANDARDS: G1.2, 1.5, 1.8
GRADE LEVEL EXPECTATIONS:	SS2, CONCEPT B2
	SS7, CONCEPT A1, B2

EUROPEAN EXPLORERS

Use the graphic organizer below to list the goals, accomplishments, and other information about the following European explorers. Answers will vary. Below is basic information about the explorers.

Da Gama	Columbus	Marquette and Jolliet	La Salle
Sailed south from Portugal around Africa and on to India. First European traveler to reach Asia by an all-water route. His discovery made Portugal a wealthy nation.	Born in Genoa, Italy. Believed that the world was round, and that if he sailed across the Atlantic Ocean to the west he would reach Asia in a few weeks. Wanted to establish a regular trade with India and China. It took him eight years to find someone to help him fund the trip. Queen Isabella of Spain gave him three ships and money. The names of his three ships were the *Nina*, the *Pinta*, and the *Santa Maria*. In 1492 he left Spain and sailed west. He sailed for six weeks looking for Asia. He reached land and thought he had reached the East Indies, but he was wrong. He did not realize that there were two continents between Europe and Asia: North America and South America. He died several years later, still thinking he had sailed to Asia.	Marquette was a missionary and Jolliet was a trader. They set out to explore the Mississippi River in 1673 in birchbark canoes. They were the first Europeans to explore in Missouri. Afraid of entering land belonging to Spain and running into unfriendly Indians, they turned around and went back to Canada without exploring the entire river.	Began his exploration of the Mississippi River soon after Marquette and Jolliet returned from their journey. La Salle canoed all the way down the Mississippi River to the place where it reached the Gulf of Mexico. He claimed all of the land drained by the Mississippi River for the French king, Louis XVI. He named the land Louisiana in honor of King Louis.

CURRICULUM ALIGNMENT		
THE SHOW-ME STANDARDS:	KNOWLEDGE STANDARDS:	SS2, SS5, SS6
	PROCESS STANDARDS:	G1.1, 1.4, 1.8, 1.10, 2.3
GRADE LEVEL EXPECTATIONS:	SS2, CONCEPT A1	
	SS6, CONCEPT A1	

THE IMPORTANCE OF SALT

Write a paragraph from a young French settler's viewpoint describing the importance of salt in the lives of settlers in Missouri.
For additional information, visit http://www.mostateparks.com/booneslick/geninfo.htm

Use Writing Scoring Guide at the back of this book.

Main points that students should mention about the importance of salt:

- Seasoning food
- Preserving meat
- Curing and tanning animal skins

CURRICULUM ALIGNMENT

THE SHOW-ME STANDARDS: KNOWLEDGE STANDARDS: SS2, SS5, SS6, SS7
PROCESS STANDARDS: G1.1, 1.4, 1.6, 1.10, 3.2, 3.5
GRADE LEVEL EXPECTATIONS: SS5, CONCEPT B2, D4, E5, F6, G7
SS7, CONCEPT A1

PLANNING A CITY: Part A

Using your knowledge of the founding of St. Louis and the necessities required for people to survive, write a paragraph describing how you would plan a city in early Missouri.

Be sure to include each of the following:
- the type of soil or region
- important geographic or landscape features
- your future plans for your city
- the name of the city
- the reason for that name

You may wish to use the maps on pages 31 and 38 in the textbook as a reference.

Online resources:
- The founding of St. Louis:
http://www.nps.gov/jeff/LewisClark2/Circa1804/StLouis/BlockInfo/Block7Efounding.htm
St. Louis history: http://www.nps.gov/jeff/1more1.htm#Top

Teachers may adapt the Writing Scoring Guide to evaluate part A of this activity.

CURRICULUM ALIGNMENT
THE SHOW-ME STANDARDS: KNOWLEDGE STANDARDS: SS2, SS5, SS6, SS7
                                                  PROCESS STANDARDS: G1.1, 1.4, 1.6, 1.10, 3.2, 3.5
GRADE LEVEL EXPECTATIONS: SS5, CONCEPT B2, D4, E5, F6, G7
                                          SS7, CONCEPT A1, B2

PLANNING A CITY: Part B

Draw a diagram of the plans you wrote about on the **Planning a City: Part A** page. Be sure to include the details you listed as important: landscape features, region, name of city, etc.

Teachers may use the Diagram Scoring Guide to evaluate part B of this activity.

CURRICULUM ALIGNMENT	
THE SHOW-ME STANDARDS:	KNOWLEDGE STANDARDS: SS2, SS5, SS6
	PROCESS STANDARDS: G1.8, 1.10, 3.1, 3.5, 4.1
GRADE LEVEL EXPECTATIONS:	SS2, CONCEPT A1
	SS5, CONCEPT G7

CHAPTER 3 ASSESSMENT

Short Answers

1. What were Columbus and Da Gama looking for? A quicker route from Europe to Asia by water

2. Who were the first settlers in Ste. Genevieve? French farmers and African American slaves

3. St. Louis became the center of the <u>fur trade.</u>

4. Who were the first Europeans to explore in Missouri? Jacques Marquette and Louis Jolliet

5. What did the locations of Ste. Genevieve and St. Louis have in common? They were both founded

    on the Mississippi River.

6. Why did the French decide to settle in Missouri? They came to trade with the Indian people for furs,

    to teach them about the Christian faith, to look for valuable metals, to make salt, and to farm.

7. Give three reasons why salt was important to the early settlers.

    a. They used it to season food.

    b. They used it to preserve meat.

    c. They used it for curing and tanning animal skins.

8. Who was the first European explorer to discover the Mississippi River? Hernando De Soto

9. How did Spain get rich from exploring the Americas? The Spaniards found gold and silver in Mexico

    and in parts of South America.

CHAPTER 3 ASSESSMENT (cont.)

Vocabulary

10. Below is a word used in the chapter. In the spaces provided, write a definition of the word, list a synonym for the word, and draw a picture that illustrates the word's meaning.

island

Definition: an area of land that is smaller than a continent and completely surrounded by water

Synonym: some possible answers are *isle, islet, tract*

Illustration: answers will vary

11. Explain how the word relates to the chapter. Answers will vary.

True or False

12. __T__ Missouri was part of Louisiana.

13. __T__ The oldest city in Missouri is Ste. Genevieve.

14. __F__ Pierre Laclede was a Spanish merchant.

15. __T__ The first settlers in Ste. Genevieve were French farmers and African slaves.

16. __T__ Portugal was one of the first European nations to look for a better way to get to Asia.

17. __F__ Amerigo Vespucci discovered the Mississippi River near where Memphis, Tennessee, stands today.

CHAPTER 3 ASSESSMENT (cont.)

Demonstrating Your Knowledge

18. How was the location of St. Louis vital to its becoming an important settlement? Explain your answer.

    Answers will vary. The main reason should be its location at the intersection of the Missouri and Mississippi Rivers. This was a good location for St. Louis because Pierre Laclede wanted to trade with the Indians living along these rivers. The rivers were the first highways and everyone traveled the rivers to trade.

19. Explain why Fort Orleans was not successful.

    Answers will vary. Sometimes the Indians that the settlers traded with for food and furs moved away from the trading settlements. Some settlements were too far from the other French settlements and places to get supplies. It was expensive to transport goods to remote places. It cost too much money to live in Fort Orleans, and the settlers could not make a profit.

20. Write a paragraph about a person from the chapter that you feel made the biggest contribution to Missouri. Explain your reasoning.

    Answers will vary. Use the Writing Scoring Guide to evaluate paragraph.

CURRICULUM ALIGNMENT
THE SHOW-ME STANDARDS: KNOWLEDGE STANDARDS: SS2, SS6
                          PROCESS STANDARDS: G1.8
GRADE LEVEL EXPECTATIONS: SS5, CONCEPT D4, G7
                          SS7, CONCEPT A1

VOCABULARY INSIGHTS

1. chandelier

    a. Definition: a fixture with several branches of lights usually hanging from the ceiling

    b. Write a sentence from the chapter using the word:
       Page 71:   Auguste Chouteau's large home in St. Louis had polished walnut floors and a glass **chandelier** from France.

    c. Create your own sentence: answers will vary

    d. Illustrate the word: answers will vary

2. cupboard

    a. Definition: a closet or cabinet with shelves to hold dishes and food items

    b. Write a sentence from the chapter using the word:
       Page 71:   Inside most French houses, you would find a few chairs, a table, beds, a chest for storing clothes, and a **cupboard** for storing dishes.

    c. Create your own sentence: answers will vary

    d. Illustrate the word: answers will vary

VOCABULARY INSIGHTS (cont.)

3. moccasin

    a. Definition: a soft leather shoe or sandal without a heel

    b. Write a sentence from the chapter using the word:
        Page 74:   The French settlers often wore **moccasins** and leather pants that the Native Americans made and sold.
        Page 78:   They also wore loose-fitting cotton shirts, blue handkerchiefs on their heads, and leather **moccasins**.
               They also wore a long cotton cape called a *pelisse* with a white or blue handkerchief on the head, and
               moccasins.

    c. Create your own sentence: answers will vary

    d. Illustrate the word: answers will vary

4. mortar and pestle

    a. Definition: a container and club-shaped tool used for grinding or pounding something into a powder

    b. Write a sentence from the chapter using the words:
        Page 81:   She owned a **mortar and pestle**, which could have been used for making medicine.

    c. Create your own sentence: answers will vary

    d. Illustrate the words: answers will vary

	CURRICULUM ALIGNMENT	
THE SHOW-ME STANDARDS:	KNOWLEDGE STANDARDS: SS2, SS5, SS6	
	PROCESS STANDARDS: G1.2, 1.6, 1.8, 1.9, 1.10, 3.5	
GRADE LEVEL EXPECTATIONS:	SS2, CONCEPT A1, B2	
	SS5, CONCEPT D4; SS6, CONCEPT A1	

FRENCH CUSTOMS

Demonstrate your knowledge of the French settlers that came to Missouri in each category below. Include details about the French and how they lived in their villages.

Answers will vary. See below for examples.

Cooking	Schools	Entertainment	Clothing
The French women were good cooks. They liked to make gumbos, stews, and soups. The African Americans influenced French cooking, as well as Indian recipes like hominy and succotash. The French raised potatoes, pumpkins, turnips, corn, melons, cabbages, beets, peas, and carrots. They grew fruit trees and gathered nuts and berries. They used wild honey or sugar from maple sap and lard and bear grease in their cooking. For meat, eggs, and butter, they raised cattle, hogs, and chickens, hunted wild game in the woods, and caught fish in the rivers.	Most children did not go to school. Free schools had not yet started. Only the richest families could afford to give their children more schooling.	The French loved to have fun. They liked music and dancing. Their favorite dances were reels, minuets, waltzes, and two-steps. They enjoyed playing games and telling stories. Everyone in the village went to the dances and parties that were held on Sundays and holidays. The French people were almost all Catholics. On religious holidays there were special family and village festivals. On New Year's Eve the people danced from house to house as they sang an old French song called *La Guignolee.* The French people also enjoyed horse racing.	French families dressed in simple clothing made by the women. Unlike pioneer women, French women did not spin their own thread and weave their own cloth. They brought their cloth from France. The men wore buckskin, loose-fitting cotton shirts, blue handkerchiefs on their heads, and leather moccasins. In the winter, they wore capotes, fur hats, and fur mittens. The women wore long red or blue cotton skirts and short cotton jackets, or a pelisse with a white or blue handkerchief on their heads and moccasins. In winter they wore wool jackets. On Sundays and holidays they wore their fancy clothes. The rich wore silk, satin, and velvet trimmed with ribbons and lace. On special days, wealthy women wore earrings, ivory combs in their hair, silk stockings, and fancy slippers. Wealthy men wore fancy coats with gold buttons and leather dress shoes with buckles.

CURRICULUM ALIGNMENT
THE SHOW-ME STANDARDS: KNOWLEDGE STANDARDS: SS2, SS5, SS6
                         PROCESS STANDARDS: G1.2, 1.6, 1.8, 1.9, 1.10, 3.5, 4.3
GRADE LEVEL EXPECTATIONS: SS2, CONCEPT A1, B2; SS5, CONCEPT D4;
                           SS6, CONCEPT A1; SS7, CONCEPT A1

AFRICAN AMERICANS AND NATIVE AMERICANS

Compare and contrast the roles of African Americans and Native Americans in the early French communities.

There are many acceptable answers. Some examples are below. Teachers may wish to use the Diagram Scoring Guide to score this activity.

African Americans

Most were slaves who helped build Missouri. They mined lead, cleared land, planted and cultivated crops, made salt, hunted and trapped, and rowed boats. Some held jobs as carpenters and skilled workers. Others worked as cooks, housekeepers, and servants. They had little freedom.

Free black men worked as hunters, rowers, and craftsmen. They also farmed. Free black women worked as housekeepers and servants. Free blacks owned property and used the courts to collect money that was owed them.

Native Americans

They traded with French settlers. They often came to Missouri to do business and to meet with government officials. They liked the guns, metal tools, blankets, clothing, and jewelry that they got from French traders. They made leather pants and moccasins and sold them to the French settlers. They also hunted wild game and sold it to the settlers.

Similarities

Both groups grew and ate Indian foods such as corn, beans, pumpkins, and squash. They learned each other's languages and sayings.

CURRICULUM ALIGNMENT		
THE SHOW-ME STANDARDS:	KNOWLEDGE STANDARDS: SS2, SS5, SS6	
	PROCESS STANDARDS: G1.2, 1.6, 1.8, 1.9, 1.10, 3.5	
GRADE LEVEL EXPECTATIONS:	SS5, CONCEPT B2, C3, D4, F6, G7	
	SS7, CONCEPT A1	

ARCHITECTURAL INVENTIVENESS: Part A

The French settlers were very resourceful people. They used their creativity to build homes that would accommodate their living conditions and surroundings. Choose one of the four Missouri regions. Using your own creativity, write a paragraph describing the features you would include in a home to accommodate the landscape distinctiveness of that region.

Answers will vary. A Scoring Guide follows the A and B parts of this assignment. Teachers may adjust scoring-guide criteria to fit their needs. Answers must reflect the characteristics of the region chosen by the student.

Northern Plains: Located north of the Missouri River. Many rounded hills and broad shallow valleys. The soil is good for growing crops. The sale of livestock is important. There are few mineral resources. Many of the largest cities are located in this region.

Western Plains: Gently rolling land with a few low hills. Located on Missouri's western border and south of the Missouri River. The land is good for growing cattle and grain. Limestone, sand, and gravel are found in this area.

Ozark Highland: The largest region in the state. It contains the Ozark Mountains. The soil is rocky and thin and is not very good for growing crops. It has large areas of zinc, iron, sand, clay, limestone, and gravel. Forests cover much of this region, providing lumber for building. Farmers raise cattle, chickens, and hogs. There are thousands of springs and caves.

Southeast Lowland: Several rivers run through this region. The land is flat and water does not always run off easily. The soil is very rich for growing crops.

CURRICULUM ALIGNMENT
THE SHOW-ME STANDARDS: KNOWLEDGE STANDARDS: SS2, SS5, SS6
                                                PROCESS STANDARDS: G1.2, 1.6, 1.8, 1.10, 2.5, 3.5
GRADE LEVEL EXPECTATIONS: SS5, CONCEPT B2, C3, D4, F6, G7
                                                SS7, CONCEPT A1, B2

ARCHITECTURAL INVENTIVENESS: Part B

Draw a picture of the house you described, portraying the features you included.

Answers will vary. Drawing must correlate with student's architectural ideas.

CURRICULUM ALIGNMENT
THE SHOW-ME STANDARDS: KNOWLEDGE STANDARDS: SS2, SS5, SS6
                                                          PROCESS STANDARDS: G1.2, 1.6, 1.8, 1.9, 1.10, 3.5
GRADE LEVEL EXPECTATIONS: SS5, CONCEPT B2, C3, D4, F6, G7
                                                          SS7, CONCEPT A1, B2

FRENCH HOMES VS. AMERICAN LOG HOMES

Create an American log cabin or a French home. Be creative in designing the structures while maintaining cultural accuracy. One suggestion for making a home is to use an empty milk carton or juice container. One way to make logs is to wrap newspaper or construction paper around a pencil or straw. Other materials you could use are paint, cardboard, and craft sticks.

You may use your book or any other reference material for assistance, including the links below:

- Ste. Genevieve French Homes: http://www.saintegenevievetourism.org/homes.htm

- Nathan Boone Homestead: http://www.mostateparks.com/boonehome/photos.htm

Teachers may adapt one of the Scoring Guides to grade this project.

CURRICULUM ALIGNMENT
THE SHOW-ME STANDARDS: KNOWLEDGE STANDARDS: SS2, SS5, SS6
                          PROCESS STANDARDS: G1.2, 1.5, 1.8, 1.9, 3.5, 4.1
GRADE LEVEL EXPECTATIONS: SS2, CONCEPT A1, B2
                          SS5, CONCEPT B2, D4, G7; SS6, CONCEPT A1

CHAPTER 4 ASSESSMENT

True or False

1. __F__ The French built their houses close together.

2. __F__ All children in French Missouri went to school.

3. __F__ François Valle II was a black slave.

4. __T__ A French log house was different from an American log cabin.

5. __T__ The French got along well with the Native Americans.

6. __F__ The first European settlers in Missouri were Spanish.

7. __T__ The food called gumbo came from Africa.

8. __F__ Most French settlers lived in stone homes.

9. __F__ A *chandelier* is a club-shaped tool used for grinding or pounding something into a powder.

10. __T__ The French were a fun-loving people.

Short Answers

11. What did the French call the porches around their homes? galleries

12. Louis Lorimier founded the town of <u>Cape Girardeau.</u>

13. What city became an important place for selling furs? St. Louis

14. French lead mining was important around what city? Ste. Genevieve

15. What is a "common field"? The field where French farmers planted their crops. The whole village owned it and each family had a strip of land in it. It was usually located just outside of the village. Everyone had to help keep up the fence around it.

16. How were French houses different from American log cabins? The French placed their logs upright like fence posts. American log cabins were made of logs laid lengthwise.

17. Why were African Americans so important in French Missouri? They helped build Missouri. They mined lead, cleared land, planted and cultivated crops, made salt, hunted and trapped, and rowed boats. Some were skilled workers and carpenters. Others worked as cooks, housekeepers, and servants. Free black men worked as hunters, rowers, farmers, and craftsmen. Free black women worked as housekeepers and servants. Free blacks owned property and used the courts to collect money that people owed them.

CHAPTER 4 ASSESSMENT (cont.)

Demonstrating Your Knowledge

Teachers may use the Writing Scoring Guide. Some key points are covered below.

18. Explain how French villages in Missouri were different from American towns. The Americans located their stores and shops in a business district and built their homes in another part of town. The French mixed their homes, stores, and public buildings throughout the village. French merchants used their homes as their places of business.

19. Write a paragraph explaining the role of French women in Missouri. French women had many roles in Missouri. They had to take care of their families. They had to prepare food. They made and took care of clothing and kept their houses clean. Preparing food included planting and caring for gardens, harvesting and preserving vegetables and fruit, milking cows, baking bread, and cooking meals. Families were large and the women had to take care of the children. There were not many doctors and the women had to look after people who were sick or hurt. The slave women worked very hard. After long days of working for their owners, they came home and had to take care of their families. French women had more say in business than most Englishwomen in the American colonies. French men worked away from their homes to engage in trading, hunting, and mining. Wives had to take care of business matters while their husbands were gone. French laws gave women more rights to take care of their property than English or American laws.

20. If you were to travel back in time to live in French Missouri, would you rather be a French settler, an African American, a Native American, or a French woman? Explain your choice.

    Answers will vary. Teachers may use the Writing Scoring Guide. Students should give valid reasons for their choice, using information in the chapter.

CHAPTER 4 ASSESSMENT (cont.)

Vocabulary

21. Below is a phrase used in the chapter. In the spaces provided, write a definition of these words, list a synonym, and draw a picture that illustrates the words' meaning.

mortar and pestle

Definition: a container and club-shaped tool used for grinding or pounding something into a powder

Synonym: some possible answers are *grinding implements, basin and club, masher*

Illustration: answers will vary

22. Explain how the words relate to the chapter. Answers will vary.

CURRICULUM ALIGNMENT
THE SHOW-ME STANDARDS: KNOWLEDGE STANDARDS: SS2, SS6
                          PROCESS STANDARDS: G1.8
GRADE LEVEL EXPECTATIONS: SS5, CONCEPT D4, G7
                          SS7, CONCEPT A1

VOCABULARY INSIGHTS

1. botanist

a. Definition: a person who studies plants

b. Write a sentence from the chapter using the word:
Page 107:   What a field for a Botents [**botanist** or someone who studies plants] and a natirless [naturalist or someone who studies nature].

c. Create your own sentence: answers will vary

d. Illustrate the word: answers will vary

2. boatmen

a. Definition: people who use a boat or work on a boat

b. Write a sentence from the chapter using the word:
Page 96:   **Boatmen** played cards and drank whiskey down by the river while waiting to begin another trip.

c. Create your own sentence: answers will vary

d. Illustrate the word: answers will vary

VOCABULARY INSIGHTS (cont.)

3. flatboat

    a. Definition: a large boat with a flat bottom and squared ends, often used to float down a river

    b. Write a sentence from the chapter using the word:
       Page 94:   For years they had floated their products down the Mississippi River on **flatboats**.

    c. Create your own sentence: answers will vary

    d. Illustrate the word: answers will vary

4. venison

    a. Definition: deer meat

    b. Write a sentence from the chapter using the word:
       Page 107:   This being my birth day I order'd a Saddle [a large piece] of fat vennison [**venison** or deer meat] . . .

    c. Create your own sentence: answers will vary

    d. Illustrate the word: answers will vary

CURRICULUM ALIGNMENT
THE SHOW-ME STANDARDS: KNOWLEDGE STANDARDS: SS2, S5,
                                           SS6, SS7
                                       PROCESS STANDARDS: G1.2, 1.6
GRADE LEVEL EXPECTATIONS: SS5, CONCEPT A1, B2, G7
                                       SS7, CONCEPT A1

THE LOUISIANA PURCHASE

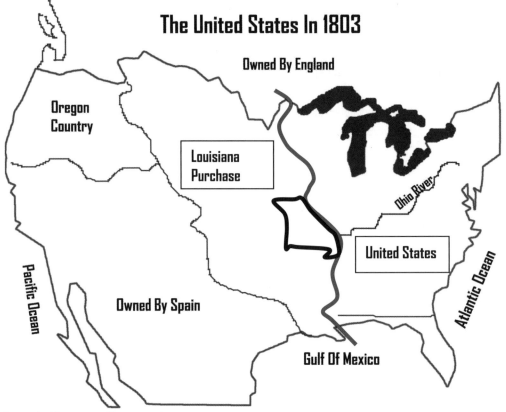

1.   Draw the Mississippi River in red.

2.   Label the Louisiana Purchase tract of land.

3.   Label the original United States prior to the purchase of the Louisiana Territory.

4.   After the purchase of the Louisiana territory, what happened to the size of the United States? It doubled.

5.   What natural landform created the border between the old United States and the new Louisiana Territory? the Mississippi River

6.   What ruler sold the Louisiana territory to the United States? Napoleon Bonaparte

7.   What did the United States pay for the Louisiana Purchase? $15 million

8.   Draw the state of Missouri in black in its approximate location on the map.

9.   The Louisiana Purchase was an important event for Missourians because it made them citizens of the United States.

10.   If the United States had never bought the Louisiana territory, what country would you probably live in today? France

THE LOUISIANA PURCHASE AND MISSOURI

The year is 1803 and you are writing from your home in Missouri to your cousin in Kentucky to tell him/her the news of your American citizenship. Explain in your letter how this exciting event happened.

Answers will vary. Teachers may use the Writing/Illustration Scoring Guide to evaluate this activity.

The basic points about the Louisiana Purchase must be mentioned:

Thomas Jefferson was president at the time of the Louisiana Purchase.

In 1803 the United States bought the Louisiana Territory from France.

The ruler of France at this time was Napoleon Bonaparte.

The United States paid $15 million, or a few cents per acre.

The purchase doubled the size of the United States.

The purchase made Missourians U.S. citizens.

CURRICULUM ALIGNMENT
THE SHOW-ME STANDARDS: KNOWLEDGE STANDARDS: SS2, SS5, SS6
PROCESS STANDARDS: G1.6, 1.8, 3.5, 4.3
GRADE LEVEL EXPECTATIONS: SS2, CONCEPT A1

MISSOURI COMPROMISE

Use the Word Bank below to fill in the blanks in the following paragraph about the Missouri Compromise. (Hint: Read the paragraph through one time before filling in the blanks and check to make sure that your sentences make sense.)

Missourians knew that citizens of a <u>state</u> had more freedom to <u>govern</u> themselves than citizens of a <u>territory</u>, so they asked the United States Congress to make Missouri a state. Each state had to decide if its people could own <u>slaves.</u> Missourians wanted their state to be a <u>slave</u> state. At the time, there were already eleven slave states and eleven free states. Many northerners did not want any more slave states. The disagreement over <u>slavery</u> kept Missouri out of the Union for more than two years. As with any disagreement that needs to be resolved, a <u>compromise</u> was made. Missouri entered the <u>Union</u> as a slave state. And Maine, which wanted to become a state as well, agreed to enter the Union as a <u>free</u> state. Congress agreed to keep slavery out of all the <u>northern</u> parts of the Louisiana Territory except Missouri. The agreement was called the Missouri Compromise.

Word Bank: state   slave   territory   slavery   compromise

free   slaves   Union   govern   northern

MISSOURI
Then and Now
CHAPTER 5: MISSOURI BECOMES PART OF U.S.

CURRICULUM ALIGNMENT
THE SHOW-ME STANDARDS: KNOWLEDGE STANDARDS: SS1, SS3, SS6
PROCESS STANDARDS: G1.1, 1.5, 1.6, 1.8, 1.10,
2.1, 2.3, 3.2, 3.3, 3.5, 3.6, 3.7, 4.1, 4.2, 4.3
GRADE LEVEL EXPECTATIONS: SS1, CONCEPT A1, B2, C3

CONSTITUTIONS

Our textbook defines *constitution* as the basic law or rules of government for a nation, state, or organized group. We have learned that Missourians had to write a constitution for their new state in 1820. You can find the Missouri Constitution online at http://www.moga.state.mo.us/const/moconstn.htm. In Chapter 16, we will be learning more about our state's constitution.

In this activity, the class will divide into groups to create a classroom constitution. Use your basic knowledge of the word *constitution* and your experience as a student to help write a constitution that will explain the type of classroom government and atmosphere you would like to have. (Hint: Brainstorm with others and discuss rules that would and wouldn't work well in your classroom. Discuss what makes a good learning environment.)

Our Class Constitution

Bill of Rights

A bill of rights protects people's rights. What type of rights would you want protected in the classroom? List five below.

1. Answers will vary.

2.

3.

4.

5.

Basic Constitution

Explain the type of classroom atmosphere you think would be beneficial to students in your class.

Answers will vary.

CURRICULUM ALIGNMENT
THE SHOW-ME STANDARDS: KNOWLEDGE STANDARDS: SS1, SS2, SS5, SS6
                          PROCESS STANDARDS: G1.6, 1.8, 1.10, 3.5, 4.1, 4.2
GRADE LEVEL EXPECTATIONS: SS1, CONCEPT A1, B2
                          SS2, CONCEPT A1, B2

CHAPTER 5 ASSESSMENT

Vocabulary

1. Below is a word used in the chapter. In the spaces provided, write a definition of the word, list a synonym for the word, and draw a picture that illustrates the word's meaning.

botanist

Definition: a person who studies plants

Synonym: some possible answers are *scientist, biologist, phytologist*

Illustration: answers will vary

2. Explain how the word relates to the chapter. Answers will vary.

Short Answers

3. Who wrote the Declaration of Independence and was president at the time of the Louisiana Purchase? Thomas Jefferson

4. Who was the first president of the United States? George Washington

5. Who was the first governor of Missouri? Alexander McNair

6. What two famous explorers were sent by Thomas Jefferson to explore the Missouri River to the northwest?

    Meriwether Lewis and William Clark

7. From what states did most of Missouri's settlers come? Kentucky, North Carolina, Tennessee, and Virginia

8. What three countries owned early Missouri? France, Spain, and the United States

9. Missouri became a state in the year <u>1821</u>.

10. Missouri's new constitution said that the state capital should be located on what river near the center of the state?

    the Missouri River

11. Name the agreement that stated that Missouri would enter the Union as a slave state and Maine as a free state while keeping slavery out of all the northern parts of the Louisiana Territory except Missouri.

    the Missouri Compromise

CHAPTER 5 ASSESSMENT (cont.)

TRUE OR FALSE

If a statement is false, write the correction on the blank to the right of the statement. (This applies only to statements marked false.)

12. __F__ Missourians moved the capital from Hannibal to Jefferson City. It was moved from St. Charles to Jefferson City.

13. __F__ The Louisiana Purchase occurred in 1903.   It occurred in 1803.

14. __T__ Daniel Boone spent his last years living in Missouri.   _____

15. __T__ Thomas Jefferson wrote the Declaration of Independence
           in 1776.   _____

16. __T__ Fort Osage was a United States military post overlooking
           the Missouri River.   _____

17. __T__ Southern states were slave states during the Civil War.   _____

18. __F__ Missouri entered the Union as a free state.   It entered the Union as a slave state.

19. __T__ Missouri's first constitution allowed only men to vote.   _____

20. __F__ The United States bought the Louisiana Territory from Spain. It bought the Louisiana Territory from France.

Demonstrating Your Knowledge

21. Write in fairy-tale form the story of how Missouri became a part of the United States. Begin your story with Spain making an offer to settlers and Daniel Boone to come live in Missouri, and end with the Missouri Compromise and Missouri becoming a state.

𝔒nce upon a time . . .

Answers will vary. Use the Writing Scoring Guide to evaluate this story.

Key points and people:

- Spain entices settlers to come to Missouri
- Daniel Boone
- Napoleon Bonaparte makes a deal with Spain to gain back the Louisiana Territory.
- the Louisiana Purchase
- Lewis and Clark
- the Missouri Compromise

47

CHAPTER 5: MISSOURI BECOMES A PART OF THE UNITED STATES

CHAPTER 5 ASSESSMENT (cont.)

Timeline

22. Put the following events in the order that they occurred in history.

Missouri becomes a state	Louisiana is returned to France
France gives Louisiana to Spain	Missouri state capitol moved to Jefferson City
Daniel Boone moves to Missouri	Lewis and Clark depart to explore the Northwest
United States purchases Louisiana	Declaration of Independence is written

A. France gives Louisiana to Spain

B. Declaration of Independence is written

C. Daniel Boone moves to Missouri

D. Louisiana is returned to France

E. United States purchases Louisiana

F. Lewis and Clark depart to explore the Northwest

G. Missouri becomes a state

H. Missouri state capitol moved to Jefferson City

CURRICULUM ALIGNMENT

THE SHOW-ME STANDARDS: KNOWLEDGE STANDARDS: SS2, SS6
                          PROCESS STANDARDS: G1.8
GRADE LEVEL EXPECTATIONS: SS5, CONCEPT D4
                          SS7, CONCEPT A1

VOCABULARY INSIGHTS

1. almanac

    a. Definition: a book filled with facts and information about weather and many other subjects

    b. Write a sentence from the chapter using the word:
       Page 126: In others there might be only a Bible or an **almanac**.

    c. Create your own sentence: answers will vary

    d. Illustrate the word: answers will vary

2. democracy

    a. Definition: a government run by the people

    b. Write a sentence from the chapter using the word:
       Page 121:   This is called a **democracy**.

    c. Create your own sentence: answers will vary

    d. Illustrate the word: answers will vary

CHAPTER 6: LIFE ON THE FRONTIER

VOCABULARY INSIGHTS (cont.)

3. ferry

   a. Definition: a place where boats carry people and goods across a river; the boat used in ferrying

   b. Write a sentence from the chapter using the word:
   Page 118:   Hannah Cole and her sons decided to start a **ferryboat** service.
                   This was the first **ferry** across the Missouri River at Boonville.

   c. Create your own sentence: answers will vary

   d. Illustrate the word: answers will vary

4. remedy

   a. Definition: a medicine used to relieve pain or to cure an illness; an action intended to correct a mistake

   b. Write a sentence from the chapter using the word:
   Page 120:   At that time Sappington's Anti-Fever Pills were the best **remedy** for malaria and fevers.

   c. Create your own sentence: answers will vary

   d. Illustrate the word: answers will vary

CURRICULUM ALIGNMENT

THE SHOW-ME STANDARDS: KNOWLEDGE STANDARDS: SS2, SS6
                          PROCESS STANDARDS: G1.2, 1.4, 1.8, 3.5
GRADE LEVEL EXPECTATIONS: SS2, CONCEPT A1
                            SS7, CONCEPT A1, B2

NATHAN BOONE SCAVENGER HUNT

Search the following web site to answer questions about the life of Nathan Boone.

http://www.mostateparks.com/boonehome/geninfo.htm

1. Nathan had more than one career in his lifetime. For what was he best known? He was best known for being a soldier.

2. What business did he open with his brother, Daniel Morgan? a saltworks business

3. According to the Historic Site Map, in which region of Missouri is the family home of Nathan Boone located? Ozark Highland

4. What was Nathan Boone's approximate age at the end of his life? 75 years

5. Nathan's home was built with a covered breezeway in the middle. According to the textbook, why did the pioneers build these dogtrots in their cabins? The covered breezeway between rooms created a cool place in the summer.

6. Who besides family members were buried on the property? There are some slaves buried on the property because they were important in operating the homestead and farming operation.

7. Create a timeline of Nathan's life.
    Answers can vary slightly. Students may opt to include the dates of the War of 1812, when Nathan served, and 1850, when he was given a commission as lieutenant colonel of the Second Dragoons.

1781	1805	1820	1833	1837	1847	1853	1856
Nathan Boone is born.	Opens saltworks with his brother.	Serves as a member of the first constitutional convention for Missouri.	Made a captain of dragoons stationed in Oklahoma.	Moves to near Ash Grove	Made a major of the First Dragoons.	Resigns from the military for health reasons.	Passes away at his home near Ash Grove.

51

CURRICULUM ALIGNMENT

THE SHOW-ME STANDARDS: KNOWLEDGE STANDARDS: SS2, SS6
                                                        PROCESS STANDARDS: G1.6, 1.8, 3.5, 3.6
GRADE LEVEL EXPECTATIONS: SS2, CONCEPT A1
                                                        SS7, CONCEPT A1

GRAPHIC ORGANIZER

Compare the past with the present by listing facts for the following four categories.

	Pioneer Times	The Present	
Schools	Answers will vary in all categories.		**Describe the Similarities in Schooling** Students are to state the similarities of the schools in both time periods based on what they wrote about schools.
Homes			**Describe the Similarities in Homes** Students are to state the similarities of the homes in both time periods based on what they wrote about homes.
Church			**Describe the Similarities in Church Activities** Students are to state the similarities of the churches in both time periods based on what they wrote about churches.
Fun Activities			**Describe the Similarities in Entertainment** Students are to state the similarities of fun in both time periods based on what they wrote about the fun activities.

MISSOURI
Then and Now
CHAPTER 6: LIFE ON THE FRONTIER

CURRICULUM ALIGNMENT
THE SHOW-ME STANDARDS: KNOWLEDGE STANDARDS: SS2, SS6
                         PROCESS STANDARDS: G1.6, 1.8, 3.5, 3.6
GRADE LEVEL EXPECTATIONS: SS2, CONCEPT A1

COMPARING THE PAST WITH THE PRESENT

Use the information gathered on your graphic organizer to write about the similarities and differences between pioneer times and today. Make a rough draft on notebook paper and write your final version on this workbook page.

Answers will vary. Use the Writing Scoring Guide to grade this activity, adding the information that is pertinent to the study of this chapter and the items to be scored.

	CURRICULUM ALIGNMENT	
THE SHOW-ME STANDARDS:	KNOWLEDGE STANDARDS:	SS1, SS2, SS3, SS6, SS7
	PROCESS STANDARDS:	G1.1, 1.4, 1.6, 1.8, 2.3, 4.1
GRADE LEVEL EXPECTATIONS:	SS1, CONCEPT B2	
	SS2, CONCEPT A1	

DEMOCRACY: A CLASS DISCUSSION

According to the Cambridge dictionary, democracy is the belief in freedom and equality between people, or a system of government based on this belief, in which power is held either by elected representatives or directly by the people themselves.

A democratic country and government is what Thomas Jefferson had in mind for the United States when he became president, as noted in his first inaugural address. Here is an excerpt from this address:

> During the contest of opinion through which we have passed the animation of discussions and of exertions has sometimes worn an aspect which might impose on strangers unused to think freely and to speak and to write what they think; but this being now decided by the voice of the nation, announced according to the rules of the Constitution, all will, of course, arrange themselves under the will of the law, and unite in common efforts for the common good. All, too, will bear in mind this sacred principle, that though the will of the majority is in all cases to prevail, that will to be rightful must be reasonable; that the minority possess their equal rights, which equal law must protect, and to violate would be oppression. Let us, then, fellow-citizens, unite with one heart and one mind. Let us restore to social intercourse that harmony and affection without which liberty and even life itself are but dreary things. And let us reflect that, having banished from our land that religious intolerance under which mankind so long bled and suffered, we have yet gained little if we countenance a political intolerance as despotic, as wicked, and capable of as bitter and bloody persecutions.

(To read Jefferson's first inaugural address in its entirety, go to http://www.bartleby.com/124/pres16.html)

After discussing democracy, its definition, Jefferson's dream of democracy in his inaugural address, and the knowledge that a democratic society encourages people to think, speak, and write freely, answer the following questions in paragraph form.

Why did American pioneers believe schools were important? What role did schools play in shaping citizens? Is this still true today? Why would a democratic society benefit from educated people?

Answers will vary. The main points should be along these lines:

- A democratic society as Thomas Jefferson dreamed about is to be run by the people.
- If the people are to run the country, they have to be able to make wise decisions.
- Schools and education help to make people good citizens.
- For these reasons, the pioneers believed that schools were very important to a democratic society.

CURRICULUM ALIGNMENT	
THE SHOW-ME STANDARDS:	KNOWLEDGE STANDARDS: SS2, SS5, SS6
	PROCESS STANDARDS: G1.1, 1.6, 1.10, 3.1, 3.5, 4.1, 4.3
GRADE LEVEL EXPECTATIONS:	SS1, CONCEPT A1, B2
	SS2, CONCEPT A1; SS7, CONCEPT A1

CHAPTER 6 ASSESSMENT

Short Answers

1. Why did many settlers want to settle in Missouri in the early 1800s? The soil was rich. Crops grew well and there was plenty of water and timber. Word spread quickly that Missouri was a rich land. The land was cheap. There was plenty of wild game and the settlers wanted to start new lives.

2. What did pioneers look for when looking for land? They looked for good land with timber. They believed that land with trees growing on it would be good for growing crops. They also needed a good water supply, so they chose land near a river, stream, or underground spring.

3. After building a cabin, what was the next thing that pioneers set out to do? They planted crops in the spaces they had cleared. For the first few years, the seeds had to planted around tree stumps and roots.

4. In what ways were the Indians' and pioneers' lives similar? They both hunted, fished, gathered wild food, and farmed. The Indian women and the pioneer women both turned corn into meal cakes and deer meat into dried venison.

5. With so few doctors on the frontier, who were the caregivers when people were sick? The pioneer women were the caregivers of the sick on the frontier.

6. The pioneers who settled in the Ozarks came mostly from the hill country of <u>Kentucky</u> and <u>Tennessee</u>.

7. Why did the pioneers prefer to plant corn? It grew well. They could make corn bread, hominy, and whiskey with it. They could store it, and they could feed it to their animals.

8. What did pioneers do for fun? The pioneers had a spirit of cooperation. They made work fun and helped one another to get tasks done. They had parties when they completed work such as house- or barnraisings. They had husking bees when the corn was picked. Women participated in quilting bees. The people got together to hear politicians. The Fourth of July was a big holiday with picnics, contests, and parades. Many pioneers loved to read, but books were very precious and many could not afford to buy them.

9. The most important place in a pioneer's log cabin was the <u>fireplace.</u>

10. The covered breezeway between two rooms of a cabin was called a <u>dogtrot.</u>

11. A country run by the people is called a <u>democracy.</u>

12. Traveling ministers were also called <u>circuit riders.</u>

13. Large outdoor religious meetings were called <u>camp meetings.</u>

CHAPTER 6 ASSESSMENT (cont.)

Vocabulary

14. Below is a word used in the chapter. In the spaces provided, write a definition of the word, list a synonym for the word, and draw a picture that illustrates the word's meaning.

democracy

Definition: a government run by the people

Synonym: some possible answers are *equality, freedom, liberty*

Illustration: answers will vary

15. Explain how the word relates to the chapter. Answers will vary.

Demonstrating Your Knowledge

16. Pioneers had a very cooperative spirit. They helped one another with tasks and even had fun while working. Is the spirit of people today still cooperative? Write a paragraph comparing the spirit of the pioneers with the spirit of people in the twenty-first century. Explain your reasoning.

Answers will vary. Use the Writing Scoring Guide to grade students' writing. Write in the information that is pertinent to your class's study of this chapter and the items that you are going to score.

MISSOURI
Then and Now
CHAPTER 6: LIFE ON THE FRONTIER

CHAPTER 6 ASSESSMENT (cont.)

17. Look at the picture of pioneers on page 124 of your textbook. How did their lives differ from those of people today? Compare and contrast the life of a pioneer with the life of a person in the twenty-first century. List three points in each column below.

Pioneer Life	Twenty-first-century Life
Answers will vary. Some possible answers are below.	
It was hard work to establish a home.	People today have electricity and modern conveniences.
The pioneers had to make or grow most of things they needed.	People do not have to build their homes themselves.
The fireplace provided the heat and was used for cooking.	People have a lot of free time for recreation.
All members of the family had to do their part.	Recreational activities are more abundant.
The pioneers had community spirit and helped one another.	People do not have to help others build cabins and barns today, but they do help others in need.
They had little free time and combined work with fun.	Working people tend to separate work from fun.

MISSOURI
Then and Now
CHAPTER 7: EARLY TRAVEL

CURRICULUM ALIGNMENT		
THE SHOW-ME STANDARDS:	KNOWLEDGE STANDARDS:	SS2, SS6
	PROCESS STANDARDS:	G1.8
GRADE LEVEL EXPECTATIONS:	SS5, CONCEPT D4	

VOCABULARY INSIGHTS

1. dugout

    a. Definition: a canoe or boat made by hollowing out a large log

    b. Write a sentence from the chapter using the word:
       Page 138   At first, they used Indian canoes and **dugouts**.
       Page 139:   Canoes and **dugouts** were too small for moving the bulky products all the way down the Mississippi.

    c. Create your own sentence: answers will vary

    d. Illustrate the word: answers will vary

2. keelboat

    a. Definition: a boat with a shaped hull and rounded in the front and back that could travel upstream and downstream

    b. Write a sentence from the chapter using the word:
       Page 139:   The **keelboat** began to replace the flatboat.
                    Keelboats were stronger and better built than flatboats.
                    A **keelboat** had a shaped hull and was rounded in the front and back.
       Page 140:   **Keelboats** also had a mast with a sail.
                    The **keelboat** could go both upstream and downstream, but moving one upstream was not an easy
                      chore.
                    Sometimes the people on one side of a **keelboat** would row with oars.
                    Frequently a rope was fastened to the **keelboat's** mast, and the crew walked along the riverbank pulling
                      the boat.
                    For many years, **keelboats** were the best way to travel up the rivers.
       Page 141:   Steamboats were larger than flatboats or **keelboats**.

    c. Create your own sentence: answers will vary

    d. Illustrate the word: answers will vary

VOCABULARY INSIGHTS (cont.)

3. sandbar

    a. Definition: a ridge of sand in a river

    b. Write a sentence from the chapter using the word:
       Page 142: A pilot had to know where the snags and **sandbars** were.

    c. Create your own sentence: answers will vary

    d. Illustrate the word: answers will vary

4. steamboat

    a. Definition: a boat, especially a riverboat, moved by a steam engine

    b. Write a sentence from the chapter using the word:
       Page 141: The invention of the **steamboat** was a very important development for Missourians.
              The **steamboat** had a powerful steam engine.
              Steamboats were larger than flatboats or keelboats.
              The **steamboats** brought many changes to Missouri.
              Steamboats hauled Missouri wheat, livestock, cotton, hemp, and lead to distant markets.
              At first the **steamboats** operated only on the state's two largest rivers, the Mississippi and the Missouri.
              When the **steamboat** came into town, people gathered to watch the boat dock.
       Page 142: Later **steamboats** traveled on the smaller Osage, Gasconade, and White Rivers.
              The day the **steamboat** came to town was an exciting one.
              When someone spotted a **steamboat**, they shouted "**Steamboat** a-comin'."
              Steamboats were beautiful and graceful.
              The **steamboat** pilot had an important and exciting job.
              He kept the **steamboat** in the deepest part of the river.
              Steamboat accidents were always a danger.
       Page 144: These items are now on display at the **Steamboat** Arabia Museum in Kansas City.
       Page 147: Suddenly a **steamboat** whistle sounded in the distance.
              Then someone shouted, "**Steamboat** a-comin'!"
              The **steamboat** was coming closer.
              He piloted **steamboats** up and down the Mississippi River.
       Page 148: As a **steamboat** traveled along the river, the boatmen would call out, "By the mark, twain!"
              But he wrote about Hannibal and his days as a Mississippi River **steamboat** pilot.

    c. Create your own sentence: answers will vary

    d. Illustrate the word: answers will vary

	CURRICULUM ALIGNMENT	
THE SHOW-ME STANDARDS:	KNOWLEDGE STANDARDS: SS2, SS5, SS6	
	PROCESS STANDARDS: G1.6, 1.8	
GRADE LEVEL EXPECTATIONS:	SS2, CONCEPT A1	
	SS5, CONCEPT E5, G7; SS7, CONCEPT A1	

EARLY TRAVEL IN MISSOURI

Outline the history of transportation in Chapter 7 of our text. Write the travel methods above the boxes (omit "early roads") and give details about the methods inside the boxes.

Canoes

Early Missouri settlers learned to use these from the Indians. They were better for travel than they were for shipping goods. Settlers could not use canoes to transport their goods and farm products to places where people would buy them; canoes and dugouts were too small for this purpose.

Flatboats

Flatboats could carry large loads and float easily down the river. They had flat bottoms and a simple shed to shelter passengers and cargo. Animals traveled on the open deck. It was a one-way craft, because it was too much work to haul it back upstream against the river currents. Owners usually took them apart in New Orleans and sold them for lumber and firewood.

Keelboat

The keelboat replaced the flatboat because it was stronger and better built. Keelboats had a shaped hull and were rounded in the front and back. There was a cabin for the crew and an enclosed area for the cargo. They also had a mast with a sail. Keelboats could go up- and downstream, but moving one upstream was not an easy chore. River currents were strong. Sometimes the people on one side of the keelboat would row with oars while those on the other side grabbed the bushes along the bank and pulled the boat forward. Other times, the crew practiced cordelling to get the boat upstream.

Steamboats

The steamboat was an important invention to Missourians. It had a powerful steam engine that turned a paddle wheel that pushed the boat through the water. Steamboats were larger than any previous boats. They moved faster and traveled upstream with no problems. They transported new settlers to the state and made it easier to trade with other places. There were dangers, though, like snags, sandbars in the river, and exploding boilers.

The Railroad

Railroads had many advantages. Steam power allowed a railroad engine to pull many cars over a set of tracks. The tracks could be laid almost anywhere. This made transportation available to parts of the state that had no river. Railcars could carry much more than freight wagons and traveled much faster. They improved transportation greatly, but were expensive to build.

RIVER TRAVEL

List the positive and negative aspects of river travel in the boxes below.

Answers will vary. Some suggestions are below.

Positive Aspects of River Travel

River travel was faster than travel over land. It was not as easy to get lost as it was for settlers traveling on land.

River travel was better than land travel for shipping goods or farm products to places where people from all over the world would buy them. It also brought products or goods from all over the world to Missouri.

River travel allowed people from other states and parts of the world to travel through Missouri.

Negative Aspects of River Travel

River conditions could force travelers to postpone their trips. During the winter, frozen rivers and ice jams made travel by water difficult or impossible.

Spring floods made the river too risky for boats. Also, lack of rain could make the river low and boat travel unsafe.

Swift currents, floating logs, and snags were dangerous.

STEAMBOAT *ARABIA*

Using information from the textbook, your creative writing skills, and the Arabia Steamboat Museum web site, write a detailed account of the sinking of the *Arabia* from a passenger's point of view.

Arabia Steamboat Museum: http://www.1856.com/story2.html

Answers will vary. Teachers may use the Writing Scoring Guide to score this activity.

Basic facts:
Students should say that they were aboard the ship during the summer of 1856 and that just before it reached Parkville, Missouri, it hit a fallen tree under the water that punched a hole in the hull. Passengers fell down from the impact, and the boat sank within minutes. No people died, but a mule tied on the deck drowned. Students may list some of the items they lost when the boat sank.

CURRICULUM ALIGNMENT

THE SHOW-ME STANDARDS: KNOWLEDGE STANDARDS: SS2, SS5
PROCESS STANDARDS: G1.2, 1.6, 1.8, 3.5
GRADE LEVEL EXPECTATIONS: SS2, CONCEPT A1; SS5, CONCEPT G7;
SS7, CONCEPT A1

CONTRASTING RIVER TRAVEL

Compare and contrast the different river travel methods using the graphic organizer.

Answers will vary. Basic information is listed in the Venn diagram below.

Steamboats

A powerful steam engine turned a paddle wheel that pushed the boat through the water. Larger than any previous boats. Moved faster and traveled upstream with no problems. Transported new settlers to the state. Made it easier to trade with other places.

Both boats transported goods and passengers.

Both boats could go up- and downstream with products.

All three boats carried goods and people on the rivers and helped Missourians trade.

Flatboats

Flatboats could carry large loads and float easily down the river. They had flat bottoms. There was a simple shed to shelter the passengers and cargo. Animals traveled on the open deck. It was a one-way craft. It was too much work to haul it back upstream against the river currents. Owners usually took them apart in New Orleans and sold them for lumber and firewood.

Both could carry large loads. They had shelter for cargo and crew. It took manual labor to move the boats on the rivers.

Keelboats

Keelboats had a shaped hull and were rounded in the front and back. There was a cabin for the crew and an enclosed area for the cargo. They also had a mast with a sail. Sometimes the crew had to practice cordelling to get the boat upstream.

CURRICULUM ALIGNMENT
THE SHOW-ME STANDARDS: KNOWLEDGE STANDARDS: SS2, SS5, SS6
                          PROCESS STANDARDS: G1.6, 1.8, 3.5, 4.1
GRADE LEVEL EXPECTATIONS: SS2, CONCEPT A1; SS5, CONCEPT D4, G7;
                           SS7, CONCEPT A1

CHAPTER 7 ASSESSMENT

Vocabulary

1. Below is a word used in the chapter. In the spaces provided, write a definition of the word, list a synonym for the word, and draw a picture that illustrates the word's meaning.

sandbar

Definition: a ridge of sand in a river

Synonym: some possible answers are *ridge, shoal, sandbank*

Illustration: answers will vary

2. Explain how the word relates to the chapter. Answers will vary.

Short Answers

3. Name four kinds of boats that early Missourians used to navigate the rivers. canoes/dugouts,

    flatboats, keelboats, and steamboats

4. Early Missouri roads were often built by road bees.

5. Pulling a rope tied to a boat's mast as boat crews walked along the bank was called cordelling.

6. Missouri's first highways were rivers.

7. A flatboat was a one-way craft on the river.

8. Which famous Missouri writer had previously been a riverboat pilot? Samuel Clemens/Mark Twain

CHAPTER 7 ASSESSMENT (cont.)

9. What knowledge did a steamboat pilot have to possess to navigate up and down the rivers successfully? He had to keep the boat in the deepest part of the river. He had to know where the snags and sandbars were, and how fast the current was in each part of the river.

10. What effect did the building of the railroads have on early Missourians' travel? Railroad tracks could be laid almost anywhere, allowing travel to places that were not near the rivers. Railroads could operate in most kinds of weather. They could carry much more than freight wagons. And trains traveled faster and were more comfortable for passengers than wagons or stagecoaches.

11. What caused the steamboat *Arabia* to sink in the Missouri River? It sank because it hit a fallen tree hidden below the water and a large walnut log punched a hole in the boat's hull.

12. What does the phrase, "By the mark, twain!" mean? It meant that the water was deep enough for the boat to go ahead safely.

13. Describe Missouri's first roads. They were difficult to travel on. They usually connected a settlement with a nearby river. Most roads were poorly built. They were rough, and after heavy rains they were very muddy. Road builders cut down trees, leaving stumps in the roadway just low enough for a wagon to travel over. The settlers then tried plank roads but these were not successful. They were smooth until it rained or snowed a few times, and then the boards would warp and rot and the roads became too bumpy to use.

True or False

If a statement is false, write the correction on the blank to the right of the statement. (This applies only to statements marked false.)

14. ___F___ Flatboats were better than keelboats and replaced them on the rivers.   Keelboats replaced the inferior flatboats.

15. ___T___ When a steamboat came to town, people would gather to watch the boat dock.   _____

16. ___T___ The pilot had the most important job on a steamboat.   _____

17. ___T___ The early settlers depended mostly on river travel.   _____

18. ___F___ Railroads could not operate in many kinds of weather.   Railroads could operate in most kinds of weather.

19. ___F___ Early roads were easy to travel on with wagons.   Early roads were poorly built and rough.

65

CHAPTER 7 ASSESSMENT (cont.)

Demonstrating Your Knowledge

20. Discuss four advantages that steamboat transportation brought to the settlers.

    Answers will vary. Possible answers are below.

    - Steamboats were larger than flatboats or keelboats, and that allowed them to carry more good and products.
    - They moved faster and traveled upstream with no problems.
    - They transported more new settlers to Missouri.
    - They made it easier for Missourians to trade with other places, they hauled Missouri crops to distant markets, and they brought goods from all parts of the world to Missouri.

21. Describe why most early Missourians preferred to travel by boat rather than on horseback or by wagon.

    Answers will vary. Some important points: River travel was faster than travel over land. Cross-country travelers had to make their way through forests filled with trees, vines, and brush. They also had to cross rivers and streams. There was often no place to spend the night, and travelers often got lost.

CHAPTER 7 ASSESSMENT (cont.)

22. Beginning with canoes, explain the historical chain of events of early travel in Missouri.

Answers will vary. Important points:

Early Missouri settlers learned to use canoes from the Indians. They were better for travel than they were for shipping goods. Settlers could not use canoes to transport their goods and farm products to places where people would buy them. The canoes and dugouts were too small, so settlers began using flatboats.

Flatboats could carry large loads and float easily down the river. They had flat bottoms and a simple shed to shelter passengers and cargo. Animals traveled on the open deck. It was a one-way craft because it was too much work to haul it back upstream against the river currents. Owners usually took them apart in New Orleans and sold them for lumber and firewood.

To make travel on the river easier, the settlers began to use keelboats. The keelboat replaced the flatboat because it was stronger and better built. Keelboats had a shaped hull and were rounded in the front and back. There was a cabin for the crew and an enclosed area for the cargo. They also had a mast with a sail. Keelboats could go both up- and downstream. But moving one upstream was not an easy chore. River currents were strong. Sometimes the people on one side of the keelboat would row with oars while those on the other side grabbed the bushes along the bank and pulled the boat forward. Sometimes the crew practiced cordelling to get the boat upstream. For this reason, Missourians were very excited about the invention of the steamboat.

The steamboat had a powerful steam engine that turned a paddle wheel, pushing the boat through the water. They were larger than any previous boats. They moved faster and traveled upstream with no problems. They transported new settlers to the state and made it easier to trade with other places. There were dangers, though, such as snags, sandbars in the river, and exploding boilers.

Missourians did try to build roads but the early roads were not easy to travel on. They usually connected a settlement with a nearby river. Most roads were poorly built. They were rough, and after heavy rains they were very muddy. Road builders cut down trees, leaving stumps in the roadway just low enough for a wagon to travel over. The settlers then tried plank roads, but these were not successful. They were smooth until it rained or snowed a few times and then the boards would warp and rot, making the roads too bumpy to use.

The invention of the railroad brought many advantages. Steam power allowed a railroad engine to pull many cars over a set of tracks. The tracks could be laid almost anywhere. This made transportation available to parts of the state that had no river or waterways. Railcars could carry much more than freight wagons and traveled much faster. They improved transportation greatly, but they were expensive to build.

CURRICULUM ALIGNMENT
THE SHOW-ME STANDARDS: KNOWLEDGE STANDARDS: SS2, SS6
                           PROCESS STANDARDS: G1.8
GRADE LEVEL EXPECTATIONS: SS5, CONCEPT D4

VOCABULARY INSIGHTS

1. apprentice

    a. Definition: a person who works for a skilled worker while learning a trade or art

    b. Write a sentence from the chapter using the word:
       Page 159:   When Kit was fourteen years old, he went to work as a saddlemaker's **apprentice** in Franklin, Missouri.

    c. Create your own sentence: answers will vary

    d. Illustrate the word: answers will vary

2. fortune

    a. Definition: riches or wealth; good luck or success

    b. Write a sentence from the chapter using the word:
       Page 156   Missouri businessmen such as William H. Ashley and Pierre Chouteau, Jr., made **fortunes** in the fur trade.

    c. Create your own sentence: answers will vary

    d. Illustrate the word: answers will vary

VOCABULARY INSIGHTS (cont.)

3. passport

    a. Definition: an official document that allows a person to travel from one country to another

    b. Write a sentence from the chapter using the word:
        Page 169: He asked the governor to give a **passport** to Charles H. Orrick.
        Page 170: My friend Mr. Charles H. Orrick is going to Santa Fe with some 7 or 8,000 Dollars worth of goods on a
                    trading expedition and he wants to get a **passport** to go to that country.
                    He is a Gentleman . . . and if you will send him a **passport** for himself and those under his command you
                    will confer a favor on me.

    c. Create your own sentence: answers will vary

    d. Illustrate the word: answers will vary

4. stagecoach

    a. Definition: a horse-drawn, four-wheeled carriage used for passengers and mail

    b. Write a sentence from the chapter using the word:
        Page 163   From there it was transported all the way to California in horse-drawn **stagecoaches**.
                    The **stagecoaches** also carried passengers.
        Page 164   **Stagecoaches** carried passengers and mail from Missouri to the West.
                    The **stage** stopped only for meals and to exchange tired horses for fresh ones.
                    Before the **stage** left Missouri, it made stops at Warsaw, Wheatland, Elkton, Bolivar, Brighton,
                    Springfield, Clever, and Cassville,

    c. Create your own sentence: answers will vary

    d. Illustrate the word: answers will vary

CURRICULUM ALIGNMENT

THE SHOW-ME STANDARDS: KNOWLEDGE STANDARDS: SS2, SS5, SS6
                          PROCESS STANDARDS: G1.8, 1.10, 2.5, 3.4
GRADE LEVEL EXPECTATIONS: SS2, CONCEPT A1
                           SS5, CONCEPT E5

PONY EXPRESS RIDER JOURNAL

Write a journal entry of a day in the life of a Pony Express rider carrying mail from St. Joseph, Missouri, to Sacramento, California. Be imaginative. Include obstacles that you encounter, dangerous situations, and details of your trip.

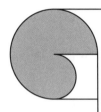

April 15, 1860

Answers will vary. Teachers may use the Writing Scoring Guide to grade this assignment.

CURRICULUM ALIGNMENT
THE SHOW-ME STANDARDS: KNOWLEDGE STANDARDS: SS2, SS5, SS6
                          PROCESS STANDARDS: G1.8, 1.10, 2.5, 3.4
GRADE LEVEL EXPECTATIONS: SS2, CONCEPT A1; SS5, CONCEPT D4;
                           SS6, CONCEPT A1

MOUNTAIN-MAN CARTOON

Using the blank cartoon panels below, create an exciting mountain-man adventure.

Answers will vary. Teachers may use the Diagram Scoring Guide to grade this assignment.

4.

1.

5.

2.

6.

3.

71

CURRICULUM ALIGNMENT

THE SHOW-ME STANDARDS: KNOWLEDGE STANDARDS: SS2, SS5, SS6
                         PROCESS STANDARDS: G1.2, 1.6, 1.8, 1.10,
                         3.5, 3.6
GRADE LEVEL EXPECTATIONS: SS2, CONCEPT A1; SS5, CONCEPT E5
                         SS7, CONCEPT A1

THE TRIP TO SACRAMENTO

How would a trip to Sacramento be different today than it was in 1860? Use the diagram below to compare and contrast.

Answers will vary. Possible answers are below. Teachers may use the Diagram Scoring Guide.

The Pony Express in 1860

The Pony Express riders made the trip in seven to ten days. They stopped about every 15 miles to get a fresh horse. The trip was through dangerous territory. There was the threat of hostile Indians, and the weather could be treacherous.

The Present

Today people make the trip in cars, planes, and trains. In cars, the trip is made over highways and interstates. The speed limit is 55–70 miles per hour. The trip is approximately 1,711 miles and if driven straight through takes 27 hours and 43 minutes. People make stops only when they need to take a break. There are dangers when driving, such as car breakdowns, flat tires, and bad weather conditions.

Similarities

The trip then and now is to the same location. People travel west through the same territory, although it has changed. Weather could still be a detriment.

TRAILS WEST

During the move westward by the settlers, Missouri became the "jumping off" place. Create a diagram below comparing the Oregon Trail, the Santa Fe Trail and the California Trail.

Answers and diagrams will vary. Teachers may use the Diagram Scoring Guide. Main points are given below.

The Santa Fe Trail: The Santa Fe trail was eight hundred miles long. It originally began in Franklin, Missouri. Arrow Rock became a favorite stopping place for travelers on this trail. Independence later became the starting place for the trail. Before the Santa Fe Trail, people in Santa Fe had no way of getting the things they needed. They did not have a settlement near them. Missouri traders believed that they could make money by selling goods in Santa Fe. William Becknell made a trading trip to Santa Fe in 1821, the year that Missouri became a state. Soon other traders set out for Santa Fe. In Santa Fe, the traders swapped their goods for furs, horses, burros, mules, and silver.   They earned a good profit on the trades they made. Missourians became famous for raising mules.

The Oregon Trail: People became curious about the Oregon country after hearing tales of mountain men and the Lewis and Clark journey. A small number of settlers wrote back home about their trips to the Oregon country, telling about the rich lands and encouraging others to come. A steady stream of settlers soon began moving to Oregon. Settlers bought their supplies in Independence, Westport Landing, or St. Joseph, and their business caused these towns to grow. The path the settlers traveled to Oregon was called the Oregon Trail. More than two thousand miles long, the trail went over mountains, through deserts and plains, and across rivers. There were no real roads or bridges.

The California Trail: When gold was discovered in California in 1848, people caught the gold fever. They sold their farms, homes, and belongings to go west. They joined the wagon trains going to California. The gold rush increased business in the western Missouri towns. The gold rush did not last long, and only a few people struck it rich. Many prospectors stayed on in California.

CURRICULUM ALIGNMENT

THE SHOW-ME STANDARDS:	KNOWLEDGE STANDARDS: SS2, SS5, SS6
	PROCESS STANDARDS: G1.6, 1.8, 3.5, 4.1
GRADE LEVEL EXPECTATIONS:	SS2, CONCEPT A1; SS5, CONCEPT D4, E5,G7
	SS6, CONCEPT A1; SS7, CONCEPT A1

CHAPTER 8 ASSESSMENT

Short Answers

1. Who was considered the "Father of the Santa Fe trade?" William Becknell

2. Which saddlemaker's apprentice ran away to explore Santa Fe? Kit Carson

3. Riders for the Pony Express could weigh no more than 125 pounds.

4. Stagecoaches carried not only passengers but also mail from Missouri to the West.

5. Missouri was known as the Gateway to the West.

6. How long did the Pony Express last? 18 months

7. Mountain men later served as guides for people traveling west.

8. What caused the Pony Express to go out of business? the invention of the telegraph

Who Am I?

9. I was born a slave in Virginia. My family and I moved to Missouri when I was ten years old. When I grew up, I lived and hunted with Crow Indians. I became one of the best trappers and fur traders in the American West. I also worked as a scout for the United States Army. My life was so exciting that I wrote my autobiography, which made me famous.

   Who am I? James P. Beckwourth

10. I organized a company to carry mail between Missouri and California. The mail was transported in horse-drawn carriages that also carried passengers.

   Who am I? John Butterfield

11. I was a free black businessman with one of the largest businesses in Independence, Missouri. I manufactured wagons and ox yokes. I wasn't always a free man. I was born a slave and made enough money to buy freedom for my wife and myself. The Civil War forced me to leave Independence, and my property was destroyed. I lost most of the money I had made in my business.

   Who am I? Hiram Young

CHAPTER 8 ASSESSMENT (cont.)

Vocabulary

12. Below is a word used in the chapter. In the spaces provided, write a definition of the word, list a synonym for the word, and draw a picture that illustrates the word's meaning.

apprentice

Definition: a person who works for a skilled worker while learning a trade or an art

Synonym: some possible answers are *assistant, student, learner*

Illustration: answers will vary

13. Explain how the word relates to the chapter. Answers will vary.

True or False

14. __T__ Trappers became known as mountain men.

15. __F__ The Gateway Arch is located in Ste. Genevieve, Missouri.

16. __T__ Charles Orrick was a trader.

17. __T__ The Santa Fe Trail made Independence an important jumping-off place for Americans traveling west.

18. __T__ Stephen Austin carried out his father's plans to invite Americans to settle in Texas.

CHAPTER 8 ASSESSMENT (cont.)

Demonstrating Your Knowledge

19. The Pony Express wanted the mail to be delivered by skinny, wiry orphans under the age of eighteen who were expert riders. Use your inference skills to determine why orphans were preferred.

    The Pony Express preferred to hire orphans because the job was extremely dangerous. The risk of death was great on a daily basis. Riders traveled through Indian country over rough and dangerous terrain. The risk being so great, the Pony Express preferred to hire orphans so that if they died on the job, they would not leave behind grieving families.

20. Describe how Missouri's location influenced people to migrate to the state and resulted in its becoming the Gateway to the West.

    Today Missouri is in the central part of the United States, but it used to be on the edge of the new frontier. Most Americans felt that the land west of Missouri was waiting to be explored. Many believed that the United States was getting crowded and that good land was more and more expensive. These people came to Missouri to use it as a jumping-off place to get last-minute supplies for their long journey to the West. Missouri also became a warehouse for products from the West. The end result was that Missouri became known as the Gateway to the West.

CHAPTER 8 ASSESSMENT (cont.)

Comparing Trails

21. Differentiate between the Santa Fe Trail, the Oregon Trail, and the California Trail. Explain why people chose to travel these trails to the West.

   Answers will vary. Main points are listed below.

Santa Fe Trail	Oregon Trail	California Trail
The Santa Fe Trail was eight hundred miles long. It began in Franklin, Missouri. A favorite stopping place for travelers was Arrow Rock. Independence later replaced Franklin as the starting place because it was closer to Santa Fe. The Santa Fe Trail made Independence an important jumping-off place for Americans traveling west. Traders swapped their goods for horses, furs, burros, mules, and silver. They earned a good profit because the goods they brought back to Missouri were usually worth more than the goods they had taken there. Mules brought from Santa Fe to Missouri helped the state's mule business. Missouri became famous for raising mules. Missourians used mules as work animals. They also sold them to buyers in other states.	The reports by Lewis and Clark and the mountain men about the Oregon territory sparked an interest in Americans to explore the northwest. The few people that traveled to Oregon country wrote their family and friends and told them of the rich land and abundance of water. They encouraged others to come. Soon many settlers began to make the trip to the northwest, and they came to Missouri to stock up on supplies in towns like Independence, Westport Landing, and St. Joseph. This caused business in these towns to boom. The path the settlers followed to the Oregon country became known as the Oregon Trail. It was more than two thousand miles long. There were no real roads or bridges. The settlers had to wade or swim across rivers with their animals; they floated their wagons across.	The discovery of gold in California in 1848 spawned a rush of settlers who trekked to California in the hopes of striking it rich. This caused even more people to pass through Missouri. Some Missourians caught the gold fever too. They sold their farms and left their jobs and families to go west. The gold rush increased business in the western Missouri towns. Each spring these towns were crowded with people ready to travel west. The gold did not last long, but many who traveled to California decided that it was a good place to live. They stayed there, and many others joined them.

VOCABULARY INSIGHTS

1. clergyman

    a. Definition: a person chosen to perform religious duties

    b. Write a sentence from the chapter using the word:
       Page 179: Missouri's new German settlers also included many skilled craftsmen, musicians, authors, teachers, and **clergymen**.

    c. Create your own sentence: answers will vary

    d. Illustrate the word: answers will vary

2. immigrant

    a. Definition: someone who leaves one country and settles in another one

    b. Write a sentence from the chapter using the word:
       Page 178: Missouri also attracted many new **immigrants** who came directly from Europe.
                But in spite of the hardships many **immigrants** came to the United States and to Missouri.
                The Germans were the largest group of foreign **immigrants** that came to Missouri.
       Page 179: Bernhard and Henriette Bruns were German **immigrants** who came to Missouri looking for a better life.
       Page 180: The Irish were another important group of **immigrants** who arrived from Europe.
                Most of the Irish **immigrants** had been farmers.
       Page 189: Living in a new and strange land was not always easy for these two **immigrants**.

    c. Create your own sentence: answers will vary

    d. Illustrate the word: answers will vary

VOCABULARY INSIGHTS (cont.)

3. stollen

    a. Definition: a sweet bread containing fruit and nuts

    b. Write a sentence from the chapter using the word:
       Page 179: They introduced such dishes as sausages, sauerbraten, sauerkraut, and **stollen** (a sweet bread containing fruit and nuts).

    c. Create your own sentence: answers will vary

    d. Illustrate the word: answers will vary

4. sauerbraten

    a. Definition: roast beef soaked in vinegar and spices before cooking

    b. Write a sentence from the chapter using the word:
       Page 179   They introduced such dishes as sausages, **sauerbraten,** sauerkraut, and stollen (a sweet bread containing fruit and nuts).

    c. Create your own sentence: answers will vary

    d. Illustrate the word: answers will vary

CURRICULUM ALIGNMENT

THE SHOW-ME STANDARDS: KNOWLEDGE STANDARDS: SS2, SS5, SS6
                          PROCESS STANDARDS: G1.2, 1.8, 1.9, 1.10, 3.1, 3.5,
                          3.6, 4.1
GRADE LEVEL EXPECTATIONS: SS2, CONCEPT A1, B2
                          SS5, CONCEPT E5

NORTH AND SOUTH

Missouri entered the Union as a slave state. Settlers from both northern and southern states came there to live. Some southerners brought their slaves with them. The Yankee settlers did not own slaves or believe in slavery. Suppose a southern slave-owning settler was a neighbor to a Yankee settler. How do you think they got along together? Do you think they sat down and discussed the slavery issue? An important part of life is getting along with others and being able to listen to and understand their point of view. With that in mind, write two paragraphs from the differing points of view of the northern and southern settlers.

First, pretend that you are a Yankee settler in Missouri. Defend your point of view against slavery. Give valid reasons that slavery is wrong.

Answers will vary.

Now pretend that you are a southern settler in Missouri from a long line of ancestors that were slave owners. Defend your point of view about slavery to your neighbor.

Answers will vary.

CURRICULUM ALIGNMENT
THE SHOW-ME STANDARDS: KNOWLEDGE STANDARDS: SS1, SS2, SS3, SS6
                                                    PROCESS STANDARDS: G1.2, 1.9, 4.2
GRADE LEVEL EXPECTATIONS: SS1, CONCEPT A1, B2
                                            SS2, CONCEPT A1

DEMOCRACY THEN AND NOW

List three activities practiced in pre-Civil War Missouri that would be considered undemocratic today.

1. Many Missourians owned slaves.

2. Women and African Americans could not vote in elections.

3. Voters had to announce their vote out loud. Everyone knew whom they voted for. There was no secret ballot.

Write a paragraph to discuss why these activities would be considered undemocratic today.

Answers will vary. Teachers may use the Writing Scoring Guide to grade this assignment.

CURRICULUM ALIGNMENT

THE SHOW-ME STANDARDS: KNOWLEDGE STANDARDS: SS2, SS6
                          PROCESS STANDARDS: GI.I, 1.2, 1.4, 1.5, 1.6,
                          1.8, 4.1
GRADE LEVEL EXPECTATIONS: SS2, CONCEPT A1

MISSOURI POLITICIANS

During this exciting time in Missouri's history, several men with ideas about democracy were instrumental in helping the state grow. Three of these men were Andrew Jackson, Thomas Hart Benton, and George Caleb Bingham. After reading Chapter 9, choose which of these men you would like to have been in this time period. Write about this person on the following page. Links are provided below for additional research material.

Andrew Jackson

The Hermitage, Home of President Andrew Jackson: http://www.thehermitage.com/
State Library of North Carolina: http://statelibrary.dcr.state.nc.us/nc/bio/public/jackson.htm

Thomas Hart Benton

Fact Monster: http://www.factmonster.com/ce6/people/A0807071.html
u-s-history.com: http://www.u-s-history.com/pages/h274.html

George Caleb Bingham

Kansas City Public Library: http://www.kclibrary.org/sc/bio/bingham.htm
Fact Monster: http://www.factmonster.com/ce6/people/A0807596.html

The political person that I would most like to be if I could go back in Missouri's history is:

Answers will vary.

The reason I have chosen this person is:

The one thing I would change in this person's history is:

	CURRICULUM ALIGNMENT
THE SHOW-ME STANDARDS:	KNOWLEDGE STANDARDS: SS1, SS2, SS5, SS6
	PROCESS STANDARDS: G1.1, 1.6, 1.8, 1.10, 2.5, 3.5, 3.6, 4.1, 4.2
GRADE LEVEL EXPECTATIONS:	SS1, CONCEPT A1, B2; SS2, CONCEPT A1, B2;
	SS5, CONCEPT D4, E5; SS7, CONCEPT B2

CHAPTER 9 ASSESSMENT

Short Answers

1. Which group of people took an active role in electing officials to run the state and the country?

    white male citizens

2. Many early pioneer farms changed into small <u>plantations</u>.

3. What continent did most of Missouri's new immigrants come from? Europe

4. Which was the largest group of foreign immigrants to come to Missouri? the Germans

5. Which immigrants were so poor they couldn't buy land and had to settle in the cities? the Irish

6. At first, most manufacturing was done in the <u>homes</u>.

7. The Missouri Botanical Garden was established by <u>Henry Shaw</u>.

8. Who was called the people's president? Andrew Jackson

True or False

9. __F__ Missouri's first elections were held by secret ballot.

10. __F__ Andrew Jackson was opposed to democracy.

11. __T__ When the Germans came to Missouri, they opposed slavery.

12. __F__ Wooden plows replaced iron and steel plows on the growing farms and plantations.

13. __T__ The subjects of George Caleb Bingham's paintings were often trappers, boatmen, and voters.

14. __T__ By the time of the Civil War, Missouri was no longer a frontier state.

15. __F__ Sauerbraten originated in Ireland.

16. __F__ The German immigrant Henriette Bruns felt that frontier life in Missouri was easy.

CHAPTER 9 ASSESSMENT (cont.)

Demonstrating Your Knowledge

17. What were the differences between Yankee and southern settlers in Missouri?

    The Yankee settlers did not own slaves. Some were farmers and others were interested in business and trade. Many Southern settlers were slave owners or believed in slavery. Many were farmers or plantation owners.

18. Characterize the difference between an election in pre-Civil War Missouri and an election today.

    Answers will vary. Some basic ideas are below.

    Before the Civil War, white male citizens were the only ones that could vote. Women and African Americans could not vote or take part in politics. Missourians attended political rallies and talked politics with their neighbors. Election day was very exciting. Many men turned out to vote. Supporters for each candidate tried to convince voters to vote for their candidate. Voters had to announce their vote out loud for everyone to hear.

    In present-day elections, everyone can vote at the age of 18. There are still political rallies, and supporters still try to convince others to vote for their candidate. Television and radio are filled with political shows. There are secret ballots, and no one knows whom a person voted for unless he or she chooses to tell.

19. Describe how the arrival of German immigrants enriched the cultural diversity of Missouri.

    German immigrants brought to Missouri their rich culture and customs. Their influence was felt in architecture, farming, foods, and various occupations. For example, they constructed brick and stone buildings. The list of foods and beverages they introduced to Missouri includes wine, beer, sausages, sauerbraten, sauerkraut, and stollen. German settlers were good farmers, and many were skilled craftsmen, musicians, authors, teachers, and clergymen.

CHAPTER 9 ASSESSMENT (cont.)

20. Explain where the immigrants came from and give four reasons why they came to Missouri.

   Most of Missouri's new immigrants came from Europe. Many were German and Irish.

   They came to America because
   - they were looking for a better life.
   - many people in their homelands were dying from diseases and lack of food.
   - their rulers did not allow them any freedom.
   - they hoped to become landowners.

Vocabulary

21. Below is a word used in the chapter. In the spaces provided, write a definition of the word, list a synonym for the word, and draw a picture that illustrates the word's meaning.

immigrant

   Definition: someone who leaves one country and settles in another one

   Synonym: some possible answers are *foreigner, newcomer, migrant*

   Illustration: answers will vary

22. Explain how the word relates to the chapter. Answers will vary.

CHAPTER 9 ASSESSMENT (cont.)

23. Imagine that you are an immigrant in Missouri in 1837. Describe the hardships and positive aspects of living in this new land.

    Answers will vary.

    Some examples of hardships could be: homesickness, missing family and friends who have been left behind, the language barrier, and adjusting to a new climate, new surroundings, and strange customs.

    Some positive aspects of life in Missouri could be: freedom, being a landowner, living free from diseases, having more food for the family, and a chance for a new life.

24. George Caleb Bingham painted pictures of frontier Missouri life and events that had meaning to him, as in his paintings *Order No. Eleven* and *The County Election*. In the box below, draw a picture that you feel represents a growing frontier Missouri.

    Illustrations will vary.

CURRICULUM ALIGNMENT
THE SHOW-ME STANDARDS: KNOWLEDGE STANDARDS: SS2, SS6
                         PROCESS STANDARDS: G1.8
GRADE LEVEL EXPECTATIONS: SS5, CONCEPT D4

VOCABULARY INSIGHTS

1. abolitionist

    a. Definition: a person who worked to free the slaves

    b. Write a sentence from the chapter using the word:
        Page 204: Brown was an **abolitionist**.
               An **abolitionist** was a person who was against slavery.

    c. Create your own sentence: answers will vary

    d. Illustrate the word: answers will vary

2. cooper

    a. Definition: a person who makes and repairs barrels

    b. Write a sentence from the chapter using the word:
        Page 208: He learned to be a carpenter, a cabinetmaker, and a **cooper**.
               A **cooper** was a person who made barrels.

    c. Create your own sentence: answers will vary

    d. Illustrate the word: answers will vary

VOCABULARY INSIGHTS (cont.)

3. cabinetmaker

    a. Definition: a person who builds cabinets, pieces of furniture, or built-in cupboards with shelves

    b. Write a sentence from the chapter using the word:
        Page 205: Free blacks worked as blacksmiths, gunsmiths, and **cabinetmakers**.
        Page 208: He learned to be a carpenter, a **cabinetmaker**, and a cooper.

    c. Create your own sentence: answers will vary

    d. Illustrate the word: answers will vary

4. Jayhawker

    a. Definition: name given to people from Kansas who attacked settlements in Missouri at the time of the Civil War

    b. Write a sentence from the chapter using the word:
        Page 206: They were called **Jayhawkers**.

    c. Create your own sentence: answers will vary

    d. Illustrate the word: answers will vary

MISSOURI
Then and Now
CHAPTER 10: A DIVIDED COUNTRY

CURRICULUM ALIGNMENT

THE SHOW-ME STANDARDS: KNOWLEDGE STANDARDS: SS2, SS5, SS6
PROCESS STANDARDS: G1.2, 1.6, 1.8, 1.10, 3.5, 3.6
GRADE LEVEL EXPECTATIONS: SS1, CONCEPT B2; SS2, CONCEPT A1;
SS3, CONCEPT A1; SS7, CONCEPT A1

COMPARING FREEDOMS

In the graphic organizer below, compare the lives of slave children to the lives of children today. List everything you know about each subject in the columns provided.

Slave Children's Lives	Children's Lives Today
Answers will vary. Slave children had very little freedom. It was against the law for them to learn to read and write. They were bought and sold at public sales and separated from their families. They had to work hard from sunup to sundown except on Sunday. They were not paid for their work. Their owners provided them with food, clothes, and a place to live. Their food and clothes were very plain. Slaves did not live well and were not happy.	Answers will vary. Children today have more freedoms. They have the opportunity to go to school and learn to read and write. Their families raise them, and though they sometimes have chores at home, they do not have to work hard on a daily basis. Many earn an allowance for the chores they do. Parents provide food, clothing, and a place to live, and often many toys to play with as well. Present-day children do not have to worry about their family members being sold. They have many conveniences and luxuries that slave children did not have.

MISSOURI IMMIGRANTS AND SLAVES

Slaves and immigrants both came to Missouri for important reasons. What were they? Compare and contrast these two groups of people that found themselves far away from their homelands.

Teachers may use the Diagram Scoring Guide.

Slaves

Most African Americans lived in the southern states before the Civil War. They did not come to America by choice. They had been captured in Africa and brought to America in chains on crowded ships. They were sold as slaves in America. They had very little freedom. They had to do whatever their owners told them to do. Families were separated and sold to other people.

Immigrants

Most immigrants came to Missouri looking for a better life. Some left their homelands because many people were dying from diseases and a lack of food. Others left to escape from rulers who did not allow them any freedom. Many hoped to become landowners.

Similarities

It was hard to leave family and friends behind. The trip across the ocean was difficult.

CURRICULUM ALIGNMENT
THE SHOW-ME STANDARDS: KNOWLEDGE STANDARDS: SS2, SS5, SS6
                          PROCESS STANDARDS: G1.2, 1.6, 1.8, 1.9, 3.1, 3.6
GRADE LEVEL EXPECTATIONS: SS2, CONCEPT A1, B2
                          SS5, CONCEPT C3, E5, F6, G7; SS7, CONCEPT B2

NORTH VS. SOUTH: Part A

In the space below, use a graphic organizer of your choice to demonstrate your knowledge of how the North and South were different.

Graphic organizers and information will vary. Teachers may use the Diagram Scoring Guide for part A of this activity.

Main points:

North

The Northern states had more cities and more factories.
Most Northern farmers lived on small farms.
They raised mainly things to eat, such as corn, wheat, cattle, and hogs.
The North wanted to place a tax or tariff on things brought in from other countries.
Northerners did not believe in slavery and many did not want African Americans living in the North.

South

Most Southerners were farmers.
Some farmers lived on small farms but others lived on large plantations.
Cotton was the most important crop.
Some farmers and plantation owners had slaves, and Southern states allowed slavery.
Most Southerners did not like the tariff. They believed it helped factory owners.

NORTH VS. SOUTH B: Part B

Using the information about the North and South from your graphic organizer, write a paragraph detailing their differences and similarities. Write a rough draft on notebook paper and your final draft in the space below.

Answers will vary. Teachers may use the Writing Scoring Guide for part B of this activity. The main points should be the same as those in part A.

CURRICULUM ALIGNMENT
THE SHOW-ME STANDARDS: KNOWLEDGE STANDARDS: SS2, SS5, SS6
PROCESS STANDARDS: G1.6, 1.9, 1.10, 3.1, 3.3, 3.4,
3.5, 3.6, 3.8, 4.1
GRADE LEVEL EXPECTATIONS: SS2, CONCEPT A1, B2; SS3, CONCEPT A1

JAYHAWKERS: A CLASS DISCUSSION

Jayhawkers did not approve of slavery and felt so strongly that they were known to attack Missourians who believed in slavery and to destroy their property. Some Missourians were just as passionate about their rights to own slaves. In Kansas, some people were even killed in the fighting over slavery, and the state became known as Bleeding Kansas.

Does having differing opinions and strong feelings about an issue give people the right to damage property or hurt others? Write an article about your point of view on this subject.

Answers will vary. Teachers may use the Writing Scoring Guide.

_____ (Name of Article)

By:

CURRICULUM ALIGNMENT	
THE SHOW-ME STANDARDS:	KNOWLEDGE STANDARDS: SS2, SS5, SS6
	PROCESS STANDARDS: G1.2, 1.6, 1.8, 1.9, 3.1, 3.5, 4.1
GRADE LEVEL EXPECTATIONS:	SS1, CONCEPT B2; SS2, CONCEPT A1, B2;
	SS3, CONCEPT A1; SS5, CONCEPT C3, D4, E5, F6, G7;
	SS6, CONCEPT A1; SS7, CONCEPT A1

CHAPTER 10 ASSESSMENT

Short Answers

1. Slaves were treated like <u>property</u> and not like people.

2. Which slave's court case decision caused a larger division between the North and South over slavery?

   Dred Scott

3. Free blacks did not have the same <u>rights</u> that white people had, but were better off than slaves.

4. Who was president at the time of the Civil War? Abraham Lincoln

5. What was the name of the new country formed by the Southern states seceded from the Union?

   the Confederate States of America

Who Am I?

6. I was a wealthy black businessman in St. Louis. I owned a barrel factory and two steamboats. I started a school for black children in St. Louis so that they could learn to read and write. The officials closed it down because it was against the law. I did not give up, but built a steamboat and turned it into a school. Classes were held in the middle of the Mississippi River and the officials could not do anything about it. My school became known as the freedom school.

   Who am I? John Berry Meachum

7. My wife and I were Missouri slaves who tried to win our freedom in court. We lost our case. Later, a St. Louis businessman bought our freedom. The court decision is one of the most famous in American history.

   Who am I? ~~William Wells Brown~~ *Dred Scott*

8. We were Kansans who attacked pro-slavery Missourians and destroyed their property.

   Who are we? Jayhawkers

9. We were Missourians who crossed over into Kansas to attack antislavery Kansans and burn their homes.

   Who are we? Border Ruffians

CHAPTER 10 ASSESSMENT (cont.)

Vocabulary

10. Below is a word used in the chapter. In the spaces provided, write a definition of the word, list a synonym for the word, and draw a picture that illustrates the word's meaning.

Jayhawker

Definition: name given to people from Kansas who attacked settlements in Missouri at the time of the Civil War

Synonym: some possible answers are *guerrilla, rebel, revolutionary*

Illustration: answers will vary

11. Explain how the word relates to the chapter. Answers will vary.

True or False

12. __T__   Most African Americans lived in the Southern states before the Civil War.

13. __F__   Slaves could own property and have guns.

14. __F__   All African Americans were slaves.

15. __F__   Most Southerners voted for Abraham Lincoln for president.

16. __F__   The Southern states contained the most people.

17. __T__   Some states left the Union after Lincoln was elected president.

18. __T__   Slaves worked from sunup to sundown on every day except Sunday.

19. __T__   The Dred Scott decision caused the split between the North and South over slavery to grow.

20. __F__   Lincoln was a supporter of slavery.

CHAPTER 10: A DIVIDED COUNTRY

CHAPTER 10 ASSESSMENT (cont.)

Demonstrating Your Knowledge

21. Explain why you think it was illegal for African Americans to learn to read and write.

    Answers will vary. African Americans were not allowed to learn to read and write so that they would not begin to think for themselves. Education and learning is power, and some white people in positions of authority did not want African Americans to have any power so that they could be controlled and used.

22. Write a paragraph describing the differences between the Northern states and the Southern states.

    Teachers may use the Writing Scoring Guide.

    Main points

    North
    The Northern states had more cities and more factories.
    Most Northern farmers lived on small farms.
    They raised mainly things to eat, such as corn, wheat, cattle, and hogs.
    The North wanted to place a tax or tariff on things brought in from other countries.
    Northerners did not believe in slavery and many did not want African Americans living in the North.

    South
    Most Southerners were farmers.
    Some farmers lived on small farms, but others lived on large plantations.
    Cotton was the most important crop.
    Some farmers and plantation owners had slaves, and Southern states allowed slavery.
    Most Southerners did not like the tariff. They believed it helped factory owners.

CHAPTER 10 ASSESSMENT (cont.)

Cause and Effect

23. Fill in the cause-and-effect chain of events that led to the Civil War.

THE CAUSE

A debate began between the North and South over slavery.

Abraham Lincoln was elected president of the United States.

Some Southern states left the Union and created their own country.

In an effort to keep the country together, Lincoln refused to allow the Southern states to leave the United States.

The first shots were fired at Fort Sumter in South Carolina, and the Civil War began.

VOCABULARY INSIGHTS

1. border

   a. Definition: a line that marks the outer edge or boundary of something

   b. Write a sentence from the chapter using the word:
     Page 216:   Missouri was a **border** state.
           A few **border** states such as Missouri did not break away from the United States of America.

   c. Create your own sentence: answers will vary

   d. Illustrate the word: answers will vary

2. guerrillas

   a. Definition: bands of armed fighters who are not a part of the regular army

   b. Write a sentence from the chapter using the word: answers will vary
     Page 222:   Bands of armed men called **guerrillas** also fought in Missouri.
           The Confederate **guerillas** wanted the South to win,
     Page 223:   The Confederate **guerrillas** attacked the Union Troops.
           The Union **guerrillas** attacked people who wanted the South to win the war.
           The **guerrillas** on both sides were very cruel.
           Some **guerrillas** and bushwhackers were outlaws who used the war as an excuse to kill and rob.
           William C. Quantrill, "Bloody" Bill Anderson, Cole Younger, Jesse James, and Frank James were all
              Missouri **guerrillas**.
           The Union soldiers hated and feared the Southern **guerrillas**.
           Sometimes the Union troops in Missouri behaved like the **guerrillas**.
           They killed and mistreated people whom they believed were helping the Confederate **guerrillas**.

   c. Create your own sentence: answers will vary

   d. Illustrate the word: answers will vary

VOCABULARY INSIGHTS (cont.)

3. infection

    a. Definition: a causing of disease in people, animals, or plants by germs

    b. Write a sentence from the chapter using the word:
       Page 227: They had no way to fight **infections**.

    c. Create your own sentence: answers will vary

    d. Illustrate the word: answers will vary

4. retreat

    a. Definition: to withdraw from danger; to move back

    b. Write a sentence from the chapter using the word:
       Page 218: Price and his men forced the Union army to **retreat**.
       Page 221: But they soon had to **retreat** into Arkansas.

    c. Create your own sentence: answers will vary

    d. Illustrate the word: answers will vary

CURRICULUM ALIGNMENT	
THE SHOW-ME STANDARDS:	KNOWLEDGE STANDARDS: SS2, SS5, SS6, SS7
	PROCESS STANDARDS: G1.5, 3.5
GRADE LEVEL EXPECTATIONS:	SS5, CONCEPT A1, B2, C3, F6
	SS7, CONCEPT A1

CIVIL WAR MAP

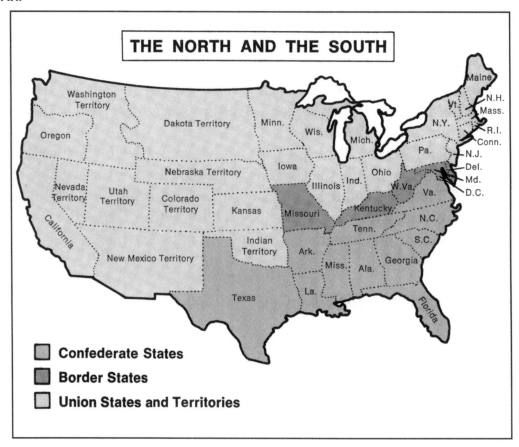

1. How many Confederate states were there? eleven **List them:** Texas, Arkansas, Louisiana, Mississippi, Alabama, Georgia, Florida, Tennessee, South Carolina, North Carolina, Virginia

2. Where did Kentucky stand in the Civil War? It was a border state.

3. How many border states were there? five

4. Where did Kansas stand in the Civil War? It was in the Union.

5. Missouri was a border state. What state is to the south of Missouri, and what kind of state was it?

    Arkansas is to the south of Missouri. It was a Confederate state.

6. According to the map, what is a likely reason that Missouri became a battleground during the Civil War?
    Missouri was a border state, and its people were divided about slavery and seceding from the Union. The North controlled Missouri during the war and the Confederacy fought to gain control of the state, which caused many battles on Missouri soil.

CURRICULUM ALIGNMENT

THE SHOW-ME STANDARDS: KNOWLEDGE STANDARDS: SS2, SS5, SS6
                          PROCESS STANDARDS: G1.8, 1.10, 2.5, 3.1, 3.5, 4.1
GRADE LEVEL EXPECTATIONS: SS5, CONCEPT A1, B2, C3, F6
                          SS7, CONCEPT B2

BORDER STATES

The border states were slave states that shared a border with free states to the north. These included Maryland, Kentucky, Virginia, Delaware, and Missouri. Slave states had to make a difficult choice: they had to decide whether to support the North or the South. Missouri became a divided state. Some Missourians wanted to join the Southern states and secede from the Union and others wanted Missouri to remain a part of the United States. Consequently, neighbors fought one another. Sometimes family members fought on opposing sides. The North controlled Missouri during the Civil War. Missouri became a battleground whenever Confederate soldiers tried to take Missouri away from the North.

Can you imagine your homeland becoming a battleground and a civil war taking place in your town? What if your family members were fighting on opposite sides? Illustrate a scene below that portrays the emotions you would feel if this were happening in your community and to you.

Illustrations will vary. Teachers may adapt the Brochure Scoring Guide to score this activity.

CURRICULUM ALIGNMENT
THE SHOW-ME STANDARDS: KNOWLEDGE STANDARDS: SS2, SS6
                          PROCESS STANDARDS: GI.2, 1.6, 1.8, 4.3
GRADE LEVEL EXPECTATIONS: SS2, CONCEPT AI;
                          SS6, CONCEPT B2; SS7, CONCEPT AI

WOMEN DURING THE CIVIL WAR

Using the diagram below, compare the roles of frontier women before the Civil War and women during the war.

Teachers may use the Diagram Scoring Guide to score this activity.

Frontier Women

The women prepared food and cooked meals. They also looked after the children and took turns staying with sick patients. The women joined the men in the fields. They made clothing for the family, as well as soap, candles, and almost everything else they needed.

Women during Civil War

While the men were off fighting, the women took care of the farms and businesses. Some women took jobs outside the home. They earned money sewing uniforms, packing supplies, and washing clothes and bandages for military hospitals. Others volunteered at hospitals, working without pay. They bathed patients, bandaged their wounds, read to them, and wrote letters for them. They also helped raise money to help take care of people who had been forced to leave their homes.

Similarities

The women were the caretakers of the sick and injured. Some started orphanages. They were hard workers and strong women.

CURRICULUM ALIGNMENT

THE SHOW-ME STANDARDS: KNOWLEDGE STANDARDS: SS2, SS5, SS6
                          PROCESS STANDARDS: G1.5, 1.9, 2.4, 3.1, 3.5
GRADE LEVEL EXPECTATIONS: SS2, CONCEPT A1
                          SS3, CONCEPT B2; SS7, CONCEPT A1

GUERRILLA FIGHTING AND ORDER NUMBER 11

Union troops in Missouri killed and mistreated people whom they believed were helping the Confederate guerrillas. In the painting on p. 223 of your textbook, George Caleb Bingham, the Missouri artist we read about in Chapter 9 of our text, portrayed the results of Order Number Eleven, which forced people in western Missouri to leave their homes. Look carefully at the painting to answer the following questions.

1. To quote a famous saying, "A picture is worth a thousand words." What do you think this painting is trying to say?
    It is trying to portray the anguish and sadness western Missourians felt at being forced to leave their homes.

2. What do you think the young lady in front of the general is saying?
    She is pleading with the general.

3. Notice the strong use of body language in the painting. What do you think has happened to the man in the foreground who is lying on his back?   He was shot or stabbed while trying to defend his home or possessions.
    Why do you think this has happened to him? He did not want to leave his Missouri home.

4. What do you think are the feelings of the man on the right who is leaving the scene?
    He is feeling despair at the violence and at the thought of leaving home.

5. What is the person on the balcony doing? He is taking his possessions and loading them on a wagon in order to leave Missouri.

6. How would you feel if you were forced to leave your home? Answers will vary.

CURRICULUM ALIGNMENT
THE SHOW-ME STANDARDS: KNOWLEDGE STANDARDS: SS1, SS2, SS3, SS6
                          PROCESS STANDARDS: G1.10, 3.2, 3.4, 3.5, 3.7,
                          4.2, 4.3
GRADE LEVEL EXPECTATIONS: SS2, CONCEPT A1, B2
                          SS3, CONCEPT A1

PROBLEM SOLVING IN A DEMOCRACY

In Chapter 10, we learned of the Jayhawkers, who felt that slavery was wrong. They felt so strongly that they attacked pro-slavery Missourians and destroyed their property. Later, when Order Number 11 was issued, some people, including the artist George Caleb Bingham, felt strongly about the fact that people were being forced from their homes.

1. How did the Jayhawkers and George Caleb Bingham differ in the ways they showed their strong feelings about issues that were important to them?

    Answers will vary. The main point is that the Jayhawkers demonstrated their strong feelings through violence, fighting, and hurting property and people, while Bingham expressed his feelings through his art.

2. In an upcoming election, there is an amendment on the ballot that you feel strongly is not in the best interest of your community or state. What can you do to express your feelings and try to initiate change? List four positive and constructive things you can do.

    Answers will vary but could include:

    * Have town meetings about the issue

    * Pass a petition and get signatures

    * Contact your representative or senator with your concerns

    * Write an editorial in the newspaper

    * Contact a television station about your concerns

    * Vote against the amendment and encourage others to vote the same way

    * Make signs opposing the amendment

CURRICULUM ALIGNMENT
THE SHOW-ME STANDARDS: KNOWLEDGE STANDARDS: SS1, SS2, SS5, SS6, SS7
                         PROCESS STANDARDS: G1.6, 1.8, 3.1, 3.5, 4.1
GRADE LEVEL EXPECTATIONS: SS1, CONCEPT C3; SS2, CONCEPT A1;
                           SS3, CONCEPT A1, B2; SS5, CONCEPT A1, B2, C3, D4, F6;
                           SS6, CONCEPT B2; SS7, CONCEPT A1

CHAPTER 11 ASSESSMENT

Short Answers

1. Explain a positive and negative aspect of Order Number Eleven, which forced people in western Missouri to leave their homes.

    A positive aspect was it might have prevented those families from being attacked by guerrillas.
    A negative aspect was many Missourians were very sad and upset about leaving their homes.

2. Why do you think African Americans fought to keep Missouri in the Union?

    The Union opposed slavery. African Americans believed they would be freed if the Union won.

3. Explain why many of Missouri's German people, such as Francis P. Blair, Jr., joined the movement to keep Missouri in the Union.

    As stated in Chapter 9, Germans had left Germany to gain more freedom, and they were opposed to slavery. They would naturally be on the side that was fighting against slavery.

4. Do you think General Sterling Price might have owned slaves? Explain your answer.

    He could possibly have had slaves. He was a Missouri leader fighting for the South. The Confederacy was pro-slavery.

5. Why did more people in the Civil War die as a result of disease rather than in battle?

    Doctors did not have the medicines we have today. They had no way of fighting infections. Even a minor wound could become infected and cause a person to die.

CHAPTER 11 ASSESSMENT (cont.)

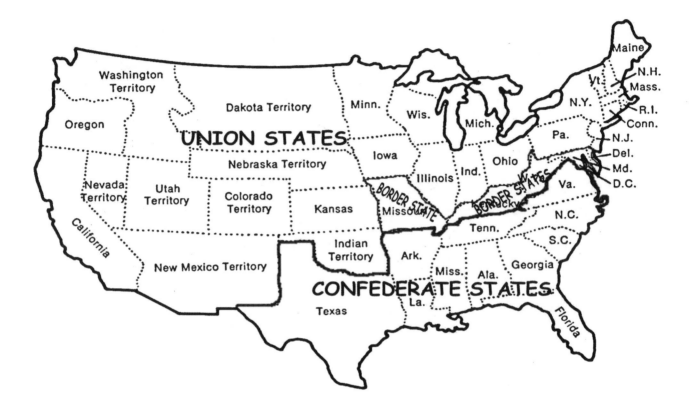

6. Shade the Border States in red and list them.

    Missouri, Kentucky, West Virginia, Delaware, Maryland

7. Shade the Confederate states in gray.

8. Shade the Union states in blue.

9. What special problems did the state of Missouri have during the Civil War?

    It was a divided state, so neighbors fought one another. Sometimes one member of a family would fight for the North and another member would fight for the South. The war tore these families apart. The death of so many people brought sadness into many Missouri homes.

CHAPTER 11 ASSESSMENT (cont.)

Vocabulary

10. Below is a word used in the chapter. In the spaces provided, write a definition of the word, list a synonym for the word, and draw a picture that illustrates the word's meaning.

guerrillas

Definition: bands of armed fighters who are not a part of the regular army

Synonym: some possible answers are *enemy, attacker, renegade*

Illustration: answers will vary

11. Explain how the word relates to the chapter. Answers will vary.

Demonstrating Your Knowledge

12. What effect did the Emancipation Proclamation have on Missourians and slavery?

The Emancipation Proclamation, issued by President Lincoln in 1863, freed the slaves in the states that had left the Union. It therefore did not apply to Missouri slaves, but in 1865 slavery was abolished in Missouri.

13. The Civil War lasted four years and left more than 600,000 Americans dead. List two other results of the war. In your opinion, was the war worth it? Explain.

Students' opinions will vary. Two main results of the war are that it brought the Confederate states back into the Union and that it ended slavery in the United States.

14. Describe the role that women played during the Civil War and the new opportunities that resulted.

Some women stayed home to take care of family members with war injuries. Many women volunteered in the hospitals to care for wounded soldiers and to help in the war effort. Some were hired as paid nurses. This gave women the opportunity to work outside the home. After the war, nursing became one of the best-paying jobs for women.

CURRICULUM ALIGNMENT
THE SHOW-ME STANDARDS: KNOWLEDGE STANDARDS: SS2, SS6
                          PROCESS STANDARDS: G1.8
GRADE LEVEL EXPECTATIONS: SS5, CONCEPT D4

VOCABULARY INSIGHTS

1. outlaw

    a. Definition: a person who breaks the law or commits a crime

    b. Write a sentence from the chapter using the word:
        Page 244: Two of the most famous Missourians after the Civil War were **outlaws**.
        Page 245: It became known as the **Outlaw** State.
                In truth the members of the James gang were **outlaws** and killers.
        Page 248: After the Civil War Missouri became known as the "**Outlaw** State."
                Governor Thomas T. Crittenden offered a reward for the capture and arrest of some of Missouri's most
                    famous **outlaws**.

    c. Create your own sentence: answers will vary

    d. Illustrate the word: answers will vary

2. bushwhacker

    a. Definition: an armed fighter who hides out in the bushes and woods and makes surprise attacks against enemies

    b. Write a sentence from the chapter using the word:
        Page 244: During the war Jesse and Frank James were **bushwhackers**.
                The **bushwhackers** raided towns, stopped trains, stole supplies, and killed Union soldiers.

    c. Create your own sentence: answers will vary

    d. Illustrate the word: answers will vary

VOCABULARY INSIGHTS (cont.)

3. Reconstruction

    a. Definition: the period of time after the Civil War when the Southern states were reorganized

    b. Write a sentence from the chapter using the word:
       Page 236: The time after the Civil War is called **Reconstruction**.
           The word **reconstruction** means to build again.
       Page: 241: James Milton Turner was a former slave who became a leader in Missouri during **Reconstruction**.

    c. Create your own sentence: answers will vary

    d. Illustrate the word: answers will vary

4. segregated

    a. Definition: to have been separated from others; set apart; isolated

    b. Write a sentence from the chapter using the word:
       Page 242: Missouri was a **segregated** state.

    c. Create your own sentence: answers will vary

    d. Illustrate the word: answers will vary

CURRICULUM ALIGNMENT
THE SHOW-ME STANDARDS: KNOWLEDGE STANDARDS: SS1, SS2, SS6
PROCESS STANDARDS: G1.2, 1.6, 1.8, 1.9,
3.5, 4.2
GRADE LEVEL EXPECTATIONS: SS1, CONCEPT A1, B2
SS2, CONCEPT B2

AFRICAN AMERICAN RIGHTS

List the liberties, rights, and freedoms asked for in each box.

Liberties, Rights, and Freedoms African Americans Did Not Have before the Civil War

African Americans could not vote. Those that were slaves could not meet with other African Americans unless a white person was present. They could not own guns or property. They had little freedom. In Missouri and many other states, it was against the law to learn for them to read and write. African Americans were bought and sold like property and they were not paid for their work.

Liberties, Rights. and Freedoms African Americans Gained after the Civil War

After the Civil War, a new law required local communities in Missouri to provide schools for African American children, though black students still did not have the same advantages that white children had. African Americans organized and ran their own churches. They gained the right to vote and to hold office.

THE OUTLAW STATE

The James gang gave Missouri a bad name by robbing banks and trains. Using information from the chapter, create a wanted poster for Jesse James and the James gang.

Answers will vary. Teachers may adapt the Writing Scoring Guide to score this activity.

Main points:

The members of the James gang were known to be bushwhackers. They raided towns, robbed trains and banks, stole supplies, and committed murder.

Many compared them to Robin Hood, who robbed the rich and gave to the poor.

Governor Thomas T. Crittenden offered reward of $5,000 for the arrest and conviction of anyone participating in the robberies or murders. The governor offered a further reward of $5,000 for the arrest and delivery of either Frank or Jesse James.

The gang was wanted specifically for:
- o   an October 8, 1879, train robbery near Glendale
- o   a July 15, 1881, train robbery on the Chicago Rock Island and Pacific Railway line near Winston
- o   the murder of William Westfall, conductor, and John McCulloch, railroad employee of the Chicago Rock Island and Pacific Railway
- o   the murder of John W. Sheets

CURRICULUM ALIGNMENT

THE SHOW-ME STANDARDS: KNOWLEDGE STANDARDS: SS2, SS6
                          PROCESS STANDARDS: G1.2, 1.6, 1.8, 3.5
GRADE LEVEL EXPECTATIONS: SS1, CONCEPT B2; SS2, CONCEPT A1;
                           SS7, CONCEPT B2

RADICALS AND RECONSTRUCTION

Radical leaders were in charge of Missouri at the end of the Civil War. They passed some harsh laws but also did some good things for Missouri as well. Create a graphic organizer to demonstrate your knowledge of the positive and negative things the Radicals did for Missouri.

Graphic organizers and answers will vary. Teachers may use the Diagram Scoring Guide. Suggested answers are below.

Negatives: The Radicals treated people who had helped the South harshly and did not allow them to do many things other citizens could do.

They did not let these people vote in Missouri.

They did not let them hold public office.

They did not let them work as lawyers, teachers, or ministers in Missouri.

Positives: The Radicals helped end slavery in Missouri.

They rebuilt schools that had been destroyed during the war and started new ones.

They opened schools for African Americans.

They established schools to train teachers.

They worked to build railroads and to make business grow in the state.

CURRICULUM ALIGNMENT
THE SHOW-ME STANDARDS: KNOWLEDGE STANDARDS: SS2, SS5, SS6
                        PROCESS STANDARDS: G1.2, 1.8, 3.1, 3.5, 4.1
GRADE LEVEL EXPECTATIONS: SS2, CONCEPT A1
                        SS5, CONCEPT D4, E5, G7; SS7, CONCEPT A1

RAILROADS AFTER THE CIVIL WAR

As we read in Chapter 7, steamboats brought many changes to Missouri. After the Civil War, railroads became the preferred method of transportation.

Using Chapters 7 and 12 as a reference, brainstorm ideas below as to why the railroads replaced the steamboat as the most important means of transport and way to travel.

Answers will vary. Some possible ideas:

The railroads helped cities grow.
The railroads helped the lumber and mining industries.
Steam power allowed a railroad engine to pull many cars over a set of tracks.
The tracks could be laid anywhere, so that transportation could be provided to places where there was no river.
Railroads could operate in most kinds of weather.
Trains traveled at high speed and were very comfortable.
Railcars could carry much more than steamboats.

Use your ideas above to write a paragraph explaining why railroads replaced the steamboat as the best way to travel and to transport goods.

Answers will vary. Students should expound on their answers above to create this paragraph. Teachers may use the Writing Scoring Guide to score this activity.

CURRICULUM ALIGNMENT	
THE SHOW-ME STANDARDS:	KNOWLEDGE STANDARDS: SS1, SS2, SS5, SS6, SS7
	PROCESS STANDARDS: G1.6, 1.8, 3.1, 3.5, 4.1
GRADE LEVEL EXPECTATIONS:	SS1, CONCEPT A1, B2; SS2, CONCEPT A1, B2;
	SS5, CONCEPT D4, E5, G7; SS7, CONCEPT A1

CHAPTER 12 ASSESSMENT

Short Answers

1. What two groups attempted to gain the right to vote after the Civil War? Did they succeed in their attempt?

    African Americans and women attempted to gain the right to vote after the Civil War. African Americans did gain the right to vote and to hold office. Women did not gain the right to vote until 1920.

2. What was the state of mind of Missourians after the Civil War?

    People who had supported the Confederacy believed that they had been right. Union supporters thought they had been right. It was difficult for them to understand and forgive each other. Each side blamed the other for the war. The two sides had to learn to live together. Radical leaders passed some harsh laws against former Southern supporters. Other Missourians tried to restore good feelings between the two sides and got those laws changed.

3. What influenced the James gang to become outlaws?

    During the Civil War, Jesse and Frank James fought for the Confederate cause as bushwhackers. They learned how to shoot guns and how to escape by riding fast horses. They learned to take what they wanted by force. When the South surrendered and the war ended, they were angry that their side had lost. They formed a gang and began robbing banks and trains.

4. Could John Wilkes Booth have been a Radical? Explain.

    Yes. The Radicals disagreed with Lincoln and did not want Southern supporters to vote or run for office. Lincoln wanted peace and the angry feelings to end. He abolished slavery in 1863 and did not want to punish the South or its people. Booth was an actor who supported the Confederacy during the war. He could very well have been considered a Radical.

5. Why is the period after the Civil War called Reconstruction?

    The word *reconstruction* means to build again. The war had taken a toll on Missouri homes, farms, railroads, buildings, and bridges. Missourians worked hard to restore their state.

CHAPTER 12 ASSESSMENT (cont.)

Vocabulary

6. Below is a word used in the chapter. In the spaces provided, write a definition of the word, list a synonym for the word, and draw a picture that illustrates the word's meaning.

Reconstruction

Definition: the period of time after the Civil War when the Southern states were reorganized

Synonym: some possible answers are *restoration, repair, mending*

Illustration: answers will vary

7. Explain how the word relates to the chapter. Answers will vary.

Demonstrating Your Knowledge

8. Explain the impact of the railroad on Missouri's growth.

    Main points:

    The railroads helped cities to grow by helping the lumber industry. Lumber from sawmills in the Ozarks was used to rebuild the state. The railroads provided a way to transport wood products to where they were needed. The railroads also helped the mining industry grow by transporting lead, zinc, and coal to where they were needed. The tracks could be laid anywhere, so transportation could be provided to places where there was no river. Railroads could operate in most kinds of weather. Trains traveled at high speed and were very comfortable. Railcars could carry much more than steamboats could.

9. Describe the positive and negative things the Radicals did for the state of Missouri after the Civil War.

    Negatives: The Radicals treated people who had helped the South harshly and did not allow them to do many things other citizens could do.
    They did not let these people vote in Missouri.
    They did not let them hold public office.
    They did not let them work as lawyers, teachers, or ministers in Missouri.

    Positives: The Radicals helped end slavery in Missouri.
    They rebuilt schools that had been destroyed during the war and started new ones.
    They opened schools for African Americans.
    They established schools to train teachers.
    They worked to build railroads and to make business grow in the state.

CHAPTER 12 ASSESSMENT (cont.)

Venn Diagram

10.   Compare and contrast the rights of African Americans before and after the Civil War. List at least three differences.

Pre-Civil War Conditions

African Americans had little freedom. They could not vote. Those who were slaves could not meet with other African Americans unless a white person was present. They could not own guns or property. In Missouri and many other states, it was against the law for them to learn to read and write. African Americans were bought and sold like property and they were not paid for their work.

Post-Civil War Conditions

After the Civil War, a new law required local communities in Missouri to provide schools for African American children, though black students still did not have the same advantages that white children had. African Americans organized and ran their own churches. They gained the right to vote and hold office. More African Americans began to earn money and own land.

Conditions that Remained the Same

African Americans still did not have the same rights as white people.

CURRICULUM ALIGNMENT
THE SHOW-ME STANDARDS: KNOWLEDGE STANDARDS: SS2, SS6
                          PROCESS STANDARDS: G1.8
GRADE LEVEL EXPECTATIONS: SS5, CONCEPT D4

VOCABULARY INSIGHTS

1. consumer

    a. Definition: a person who buys and uses a product

    b. Write a sentence from the chapter using the word:
       Page 267: They were now **consumers**.

    c. Create your own sentence: answers will vary

    d. Illustrate the word: answers will vary

2. fertilizer

    a. Definition: something added to the soil to make it produce more crops

    b. Write a sentence from the chapter using the word:
       Page 263: They used new **fertilizers** and better kinds of seeds.

    c. Create your own sentence: answers will vary

    d. Illustrate the word: answers will vary

VOCABULARY INSIGHTS (cont.)

3. kerosene

    a. Definition: a thin oil sometimes used for burning in a cooking stove, lamp, or heater

    b. Write a sentence from the chapter using the word:
       Page 256:   Before his invention, people lighted their homes and businesses with **kerosene** lamps or candles.
       Pages 267–68: There were also barrels of vinegar, **kerosene**, and molasses.

    c. Create your own sentence: answers will vary

    d. Illustrate the word: answers will vary

4. licorice

    a. Definition: a black, sweet-tasting, gummy extract from a plant; candy flavored with this extract

    b. Write a sentence from the chapter using the word:
       Page 268: Stick candy and **licorice** were popular with children.

    c. Create your own sentence: answers will vary

    d. Illustrate the word: answers will vary

CURRICULUM ALIGNMENT

THE SHOW-ME STANDARDS: KNOWLEDGE STANDARDS: MA1, SS2, SS5
PROCESS STANDARDS: G1.2, 3.1, 3.3
GRADE LEVEL EXPECTATIONS: SS2, CONCEPT A1
SS5, CONCEPT B2

AUTOMOBILES

The first automobiles were very different from the cars of today, as were road conditions. The first cars had to travel on narrow dirt roads and often got stuck in the mud. They could not go very fast. The Missouri General Assembly passed a law to set the speed limit at 9 miles per hour. Determine how long it would have taken you to drive to the St. Louis World's Fair from the following locations.

Starting from:	Miles to St. Louis	Approximate travel time @ 9 mph
Kansas City	234 miles	_26_ hours
Hannibal	99 miles	_11_ hours
Springfield	198 miles	_22_ hours
Poplar Bluff	135 miles	_15_ hours
Jefferson City	108 miles	_12_ hours
Warrensburg	189 miles	_21_ hours
Joplin	252 miles	_28_ hours
Smithville	234 miles	_26_ hours
Kennett	171 miles	_19_ hours
West Plains	153 miles	_17_ hours

CURRICULUM ALIGNMENT

THE SHOW-ME STANDARDS: KNOWLEDGE STANDARDS: SS2, SS6
                         PROCESS STANDARDS: G1.2, 1.8, 1.10,
                         2.5
GRADE LEVEL EXPECTATIONS: SS2, CONCEPT A1
                         SS7, CONCEPT A1

POSTCARD FROM THE ST. LOUIS WORLD'S FAIR

On the postcard below, write a message to your aunt in Kansas City inviting her to come to St. Louis to join you at the World's Fair. Describe some of the new and exciting things she will see there.

Answers and illustrations will vary. Teachers may adapt the Writing Scoring Guide to score this activity.

Design the front of your postcard with some of the images you described from the World's Fair.

CURRICULUM ALIGNMENT

THE SHOW-ME STANDARDS: KNOWLEDGE STANDARDS: SS2
                          PROCESS STANDARDS: G1.8, 1.10, 4.1
GRADE LEVEL EXPECTATIONS: SS2, CONCEPT A1
                          SS7, CONCEPT A1

INVENTIONS

Many new inventions after the Civil War brought changes to the way Missourians lived, worked, and played. Circle one of the inventions below and explain in paragraph form how your life would be different today if it had not been invented.

lightbulb   camera   toilet   hot and cold running water   automobile

vacuum cleaner   electric iron   phonograph   bathtub   telephone

Answers will vary. Teachers may use the Writing Scoring Guide to score this activity.

CURRICULUM ALIGNMENT
THE SHOW-ME STANDARDS: KNOWLEDGE STANDARDS: SS2, SS6
                          PROCESS STANDARDS: G1.5, 1.6
GRADE LEVEL EXPECTATIONS: SS2, CONCEPT A1

LOUISIANA PURCHASE/WORLD'S FAIR

Read the paragraphs and fill in the blanks using the words in the Word Bank below.

The Louisiana Purchase <u>Exposition</u>, also known as the 1904 World's Fair, was held to commemorate the 100th anniversary of the Louisiana <u>Purchase</u> from the French ruler, <u>Napoleon</u>, by the United States. The purchase of the Louisiana Territory <u>doubled</u> the size of the United States. It included the land that we now know as the states of Arkansas, Oklahoma, Missouri, Kansas, Nebraska, Iowa, North and South Dakota, and Montana, and parts of Minnesota, Wyoming, and Colorado. The Louisiana Territory covered all the land between the <u>Mississippi</u> River and the Rocky <u>Mountains</u>. The land deal cost the United States <u>fifteen</u> million dollars, which amounted to only a few <u>cents</u> an acre.

The 1904 World's Fair was a spectacular event that took six years to build. Originally, the fair was due to open a year earlier, but it ran behind schedule and was delayed until 1904. Many new <u>inventions</u> were introduced at the fair. The fairgrounds covered more than twelve hundred <u>acres</u>. More than 12 million people from all over the world came to the fair to celebrate the anniversary of the Louisiana Purchase.

Word Bank:

Mississippi	doubled	Purchase	inventions	cents
Exposition	acres	Napoleon	fifteen	Mountains

CURRICULUM ALIGNMENT
THE SHOW-ME STANDARDS: KNOWLEDGE STANDARDS: SS2, SS6
                          PROCESS STANDARDS: G1.1, 1.5, 1.6, 1.10, 2.5, 3.5, 4.1
GRADE LEVEL EXPECTATIONS: SS2, CONCEPT A1, B2;
                          SS5, CONCEPT D4, E5, F6, G7; SS7, CONCEPT B2

GROWTH OF MISSOURI CITIES

Many people moved to Missouri cities after the Civil War. Explain why people moved from farms and small towns into large cities and what was responsible for the growth of cities.

The more people that moved to Missouri, the more products were needed. This need could not be met by small workshops, so the small shops grew into factories. The new factories needed more people. Workers began to move to the cities to get jobs in the factories. Every year the number of factory workers grew.

In the space below, draw a picture of St. Louis as it may have looked before the Civil War.

Drawings should depict workshops, small towns, etc., and few—if any—factories,

In the space below, draw a picture of St. Louis as it may have looked after the Civil War.

Drawings should depict cities with factories, buildings, and more people than in the pre-Civil War drawing above.

123

WOMEN, THEN AND NOW

Write a paragraph comparing society's expectations of a young girl in 1904 with society's expectations of girls today. Discuss employment, careers, education, and rights. Brainstorm your ideas on a separate sheet of paper and write your final draft below.

Answers will vary. Teachers may use the Writing Scoring Guide. Suggested answers are below.

1904: Most women stayed at home taking care of their families. A number of women, especially those who were poor or unmarried, went to work outside the home. Some went to work in the factories, making cigars, shoes, and clothing. All working women were paid less than men with the same jobs. Some women took jobs as servants and housekeepers. In the cities, women worked as telephone operators and as sales clerks in department stores. More girls began to attend high school and college. Two professions open to women were teaching and nursing. A few women became doctors and lawyers. They faced many hardships, as most people did not believe that women should have these roles. Women still did not have the right to vote.

Today: Many more women work outside the home today than in 1904, whether they are married or unmarried, wealthy or poor. Women today work in all professions, from doctors and lawyers to factory workers and housekeepers. Women are compensated monetarily better today and in most cases receive the same salary as a man in the same position. Most girls attend high school and college. Society today is much more receptive to female doctors and lawyers. Women gained the right to vote in 1920, and women vote and run for office in today's society.

CURRICULUM ALIGNMENT

THE SHOW-ME STANDARDS: KNOWLEDGE STANDARDS: SS6
                         PROCESS STANDARDS: G1.2, 1.4, 1.8, 1.10
GRADE LEVEL EXPECTATIONS: SS2, CONCEPT A1
                         SS7, CONCEPT B2

GEORGE WASHINGTON CARVER

Read about the life and accomplishments of this famous Missourian at http://www.nps.gov/gwca/expanded/gwc.htm. Create a story in the boxes below using the most important events in his life. Answers will vary. Teachers may use the Diagram Scoring Guide to score this assignment.

4.

1.

5.

2.

6.

3.

125

CHAPTER 13 ASSESSMENT

Short Answers

1. What impact did George Washington Carver have on Missouri?

    He was a famous teacher and scientist who was known for his research on peanuts, sweet potatoes, and other foods. He made important discoveries in agriculture. He also worked to improve relations between the races.

2. Why did people move into the cities in Missouri in the years after the Civil War?

    More people moved to Missouri, and the need for products rose with the population. Small workshops became factories in order to produce the amount of products needed. Most of the new factories were built in cities. The factories needed more workers. People moved from farms and small towns into the large cities to work in the factories. Each year the number of factories grew.

3. The St. Louis World's Fair was held to commemorate the 100th anniversary of what event?

    the Louisiana Purchase

4. List the different kinds of progress that farmers achieved in Missouri in the years after the Civil War.

    Farmers began using more machines after the Civil War. Some of these were corn planters, binders, threshing machines, hay balers, corn shellers, and plows with wheels and a seat for the driver. Horses and mules still pulled most of these new machines, but a few were run by steam engines. Farmers began to use new fertilizers and better kinds of seeds. Missouri's most important crops were corn, wheat, barley, tobacco, hay, fruit, and vegetables. Farmers also raised cattle, hogs, horses, mules, sheep, and chicken.

Demonstrating Your Knowledge

5. Summarize the changes in women's roles in society since 1904.

    Many more women work outside the home today than in 1904, whether they are married or unmarried, wealthy or poor. Women today work in all professions, from doctors and lawyers to factory workers and housekeepers. Women are compensated financially better today than in the past and in most cases receive the same salary as men in the same position. Most girls attend high school and college. Society today is much more receptive to female doctors and lawyers. Women gained the right to vote in 1920, and women vote and run for office in today's society.

6. Choose three inventions from the chapter and describe the effect they had on Missourians' lives.

    Answers will vary. Students should list improvements in quality of life that stemmed from the following inventions: electric lightbulb, telephone, phonograph, camera, vacuum cleaner, electric iron, indoor toilets, bathtubs, hot and cold running water, and automobiles.

CHAPTER 13 ASSESSMENT (cont.)

Vocabulary

7.   Below is a word used in the chapter. In the spaces provided, write a definition of the word, list a synonym for the word, and draw a picture that illustrates the word's meaning.

consumer

Definition: a person who buys and uses a product

Synonym: some possible answers are *customer, buyer, shopper*

Illustration: answers will vary

8.   Explain how the word relates to the chapter. Answers will vary.

Demonstrating Your Knowledge

9.   Differentiate between department stores and general stores.

Answers will vary. Some main points follow.

Department stores were in large buildings; they sometimes filled an entire city block. They sold many different kinds of goods. There was a separate department for each kind of goods. Each department had its own salespeople. Department stores sold ready-made clothing in different sizes. They also sold furniture, household goods, and many other items. They used glass cases, mirrors, and colorful decorations to attract shoppers. They also provided restrooms and restaurants for their customers. Department stores were found in larger cities and towns.

General stores were found in small towns. They were one-room buildings lined with shelves. The food was on one side of the store. and dry goods were kept behind the counter. Smaller metal cans held salt, pepper, and spices. Wooden kegs contained butter, pickles, and chewing tobacco. There were also barrels of vinegar, kerosene, and molasses. The clerk would measure the requested amount from these containers. There was a glass candy counter filled with many kinds of candy. General stores also sold tools and household goods. Shelves were filled with cloth, shoes, and clothing. General stores opened very early in the morning and stayed open until their last customer left in the evening. The general store was also a meeting place where men could gather to swap stories and the latest news. Women visited while they selected the things they needed.

CHAPTER 13 ASSESSMENT (cont.)

10. List five things a visitor might have seen at the Louisiana Purchase Exposition. Give details.

    Answers will vary. Some of the sights that could have been seen at the fair were:

    - People from all over the world.
    - Sixty-two different nations' displays telling about their countries. Every state except Delaware had a building to show things at the fair.
    - Fairgrounds covering more than twelve hundred acres.
    - Thousands of electric lightbulbs lighting the fairgrounds.
    - The Pike, a long street lined on both sides with amusement rides and exhibits.
    - A funhouse with slides, turning barrels, funny mirrors, and roller coasters.
    - A Ferris wheel that was 260 feet high with thirty-six cars, each car holding sixty people.
    - A hot air balloon.
    - A Wild West show with Indian people dressed in tribal costumes.
    - A wild animal show.
    - A man mounted on a horse diving from a high cliff into a pool of water.
    - Many restaurants and concession stands.
    - A waffle maker making some of the first ice-cream cones in America.
    - A building with tanks of fish and seahorses.
    - A Japanese garden.
    - A Swiss mountain village.
    - Birds in a giant birdcage that is still used today at the St. Louis Zoo in Forest Park.
    - The Palace of Electricity, which was filled with new electrical inventions.
    - Waterfalls and fountains pouring into a lagoon.

VOCABULARY INSIGHTS

1. commander

   a. Definition: a person in charge of an army, ship, or camp; a ruler or leader

   b. Write a sentence from the chapter using the word:
      Page 283: He was the **commander** of all American troops in Europe.

   c. Create your own sentence: answers will vary

   d. Illustrate the word: answers will vary

2. depression

   a. Definition: a period of time in which business is slow and many people are out of work

   b. Write a sentence from the chapter using the word:
      Page 279: During the 1930s there was the Great **Depression**.
      Page 288: Such bad times are called a **depression**.
                The Great **Depression** beginning in 1929 seemed to get worse and worse.
                During the Great **Depression** these workers were put to work building sidewalks in St. Louis.
      Page 289: The Great **Depression** years were very hard for the Mays.
                Because of the **depression** he could not find work much of the time.
      Page 290: Cleo was homesick some of the time, but he was glad to have a job during the Great **Depression**.
      Page 291: Many years later, their sister Rowena wrote a book about her family and the Great **Depression**.
      Page 292: The Great **Depression** was hard on most Missourians.
      Page 294: These and many other wonderful Missouri athletes and entertainers helped all Americans get through
                the hard times of the Great **Depression** years.

   c. Create your own sentence: answers will vary

   d. Illustrate the word: answers will vary

VOCABULARY INSIGHTS (cont.)

3. submarine

    a. Definition: a boat that can operate underwater

    b. Write a sentence from the chapter using the word:
       Page 279: Powerful new weapons such as the **submarine**, the machine gun, and poison gas changed the way wars were fought.
       The Germans called these boats U-boats, but today we call them **submarines**.

    c. Create your own sentence: answers will vary

    d. Illustrate the word: answers will vary

4. victory

    a. Definition: the defeat of an enemy in combat or war; success in a contest

    b. Write a sentence from the chapter using the word:
       Page 283: The Americans celebrated the **victory.**

    c. Create your own sentence: answers will vary

    d. Illustrate the word: answers will vary

CURRICULUM ALIGNMENT

THE SHOW-ME STANDARDS: KNOWLEDGE STANDARDS: SS2, SS6, SS7
PROCESS STANDARDS: G1.6, 1.8, 1.10, 3.1
GRADE LEVEL EXPECTATIONS: SS2, CONCEPT A1; SS3, CONCEPT A1;
SS6, CONCEPT A1; SS7, CONCEPT A1

BLACK MISSOURIANS AFTER WORLD WAR I

Write a paragraph about the situation of African Americans in Missouri after World War I. Describe the strides that African Americans made to pave the way for others and end segregation in Missouri. You may use the lives of specific African Americans' as examples.

Brainstorm your ideas and write a rough draft on notebook paper. Write your final draft below.

Answers will vary. Teachers may use the Writing Scoring Guide. Suggested content ideas are below.

Situation of African Americans:

Black Missourians were allowed to vote. In 1921 Missouri voters elected the first black member of the Missouri General Assembly. But Missouri was still a segregated state. There were separate schools for blacks. African Americans could not stay at most hotels. Most restaurants served only whites. Many African American leaders worked to end segregation.

Specific lives as examples of progress made:

Homer G. Phillips was an important African American lawyer and politician. He had to leave the state to study the law because no law schools were open to black students. He graduated from the Howard University law school in Washington, D.C. He opened a law office in St. Louis, where he became a community leader and worked for civil rights. He also worked to have a hospital built to serve the black community.

Lloyd Gaines was another African American who tried to make things better for black Missourians. He also wanted to attend law school, but didn't want to leave the state. The United States Supreme Court told Missouri to either let him attend the University of Missouri law school or set up a separate law school for black students. This made it clear that Missouri would have to make changes in its treatment of African Americans.

Lucile Bluford also fought to end segregation in Missouri. She went to the courts to try to get admitted to the Journalism School at the University of Missouri. She did not get to attend the university, but she became a leader in the Civil Rights movement. The governor chose her to be one of the first members of the Missouri Commission on Human Rights. She was also a leader of the National Association for the Advancement of Colored People, and she became editor of the *Kansas City Call.* Fifty years after she tried to enroll at the University of Missouri, the school gave her an honorary doctor's degree.

CURRICULUM ALIGNMENT
THE SHOW-ME STANDARDS: KNOWLEDGE STANDARDS: SS2,
                                                    SS5, SS6
                                            PROCESS STANDARDS: G1.2, 1.6,
                                                    1.8, 1.9, 1.10, 3.1
GRADE LEVEL EXPECTATIONS: SS2, CONCEPT A1; SS7, CONCEPT A1

COMPARING THE DEPRESSION WITH THE PRESENT

Times were hard during the Great Depression. People had to make things last and be creative to survive. But Missourians are very resilient people.

Explain how Thomas and Lulah May, the couple described in your textbook, provided food, clothing, and toys for their family during the Great Depression.

Food	Clothing	Toys
The Mays had very little money to spend, and often did not have enough to eat. The only groceries that they bought during the depression were flour, sugar, salt, dry beans, baking powder, lard, coffee, vinegar, and cocoa. They had to provide everything else they ate. They raised a garden and ate mushrooms, dandelions, and other wild plants. The men hunted and fished for meat. The women canned vegetables, fruit, and meat in glass jars in order to have food in the winter.	During the depression, the Mays could not afford to buy clothes. Lulah May sewed the family's clothes. She often made them from used clothes that other people gave them. They bought their shoes from the Sears and Roebuck catalog.	The children had only homemade toys. They made dolls and stuffed animals from socks, using buttons to make the eyes. They also made toys from wooden thread spools.

Describe how your family provides food, clothing, and toys.

Food	Clothing	Toys
Answers will vary. Mothers and fathers work to provide food for their families. Some people hunt and grow gardens for food, but they do not depend on those methods as heavily as did families during the depression. Families today buy food at grocery stores, and many eat at restaurants and fast-food places. Food is abundant, and most children and families get to eat as much as they want and rarely go hungry.	Today families buy most of their clothing and shoes from department or discount stores. Few people sew their clothes, and very few families make all their own clothing. Children have many more clothes than children during the depression had. Moreover, their clothing can be very expensive depending on the label or maker.	Children today get their toys from stores. They receive toys more often than depression children. Toys today can be very expensive. There is a wide variety of toys, from dolls to sports gear to technological equipment.

MISSOURI
Then and Now
CHAPTER 14: SOME GOOD TIMES AND BAD TIMES

CURRICULUM ALIGNMENT
THE SHOW-ME STANDARDS: KNOWLEDGE STANDARDS: SS2, SS6, SS7
PROCESS STANDARDS: G1.1, 1.6, 1.9, 2.4,
3.1, 3.5, 4.1, 4.2
GRADE LEVEL EXPECTATIONS: SS2, CONCEPT A1
SS4, CONCEPT D4

VOLUNTEERISM IN MISSOURI

Look carefully at the poster on page 280 of your textbook. What do you think the United States Food Administration was encouraging Missouri citizens to do? What is meant by the slogan, "Food Is Ammunition - Don't Waste It?"

Answers will vary. Suggested answers are below.

The United States Food Administration was encouraging Missourians to conserve food to help feed America and its allies in Europe during the war. The slogan encouraged families not to waste anything, because the troops and the citizens at home needed to be well fed and healthy.

List three ways in which Missourians helped the war effort.

- Many Missourians joined the army and navy.
- Women worked as volunteers in Red Cross canteens in Europe.
- Farmers raised extra food to help feed America and its allies in Europe.
- Many Missourians ate less sugar and meat, to conserve it for the war effort.
- Workers in Missouri's factories produced clothing, shoes, chemicals, weapons, machinery, and other things needed to fight the war.

CURRICULUM ALIGNMENT

THE SHOW-ME STANDARDS: KNOWLEDGE STANDARDS: SS2, SS6
                         PROCESS STANDARDS: G1.2, 1.6,
                         1.8, 1.9
GRADE LEVEL EXPECTATIONS: SS2, CONCEPT AI
                         SS7, CONCEPT AI

POSTWAR MISSOURI

Compare the progress made in Missouri after the Civil War with the progress made after World War I. What are the similarities? What was the frame of mind of Missourians after these wars? Demonstrate your knowledge in the graphic organizer below.

Post-Civil War Missouri (1865)	Post-World War I Missouri (1920s)	Similarities
Economic Progress Missourians worked hard to rebuild the state after the war. Farmers began raising more crops than before the war, and more people came to Missouri to live. Stores, factories, and businesses that had been closed by the war were reopened. The state began growing with new businesses being opened and the building of new railroads.	**Economic Progress** Most people had jobs. They could afford to buy appliances, phonographs, radios, and other new inventions. Some bought automobiles, which led to the establishment of new businesses for travelers. In addition to listening to the radio and traveling in their cars, many people went to the movies.	**Economic Progress** Answers will vary. Job employment went up as people began to put the wars behind them. The state began growing after each of the wars.
Transportation Railroads were the best way to travel and transport goods. People rode horses and used wagons and steamboats.	**Transportation** Many people bought their first automobile, and Missouri organized the State Highway Patrol. Charles Lindbergh flew a one-engine airplane from New York to Paris without stopping. St. Louis became a major center for airplanes.	**Transportation** Answers will vary. The railroad was operating during both war periods. Horses were still in use during World War I, but they were not used as much as they were during the Civil War period.
Postwar Frame of Mind Missourians worked hard to rebuild the state after the war. Radicals passed some harsh laws against people who had helped the South during the war. Other Missourians wanted to restore good feelings and worked to get those laws changed—and they did.	**Postwar Frame of Mind** People wanted things to be the way they were before the war. The 1920s were good times for most Missourians. Most people had jobs and could afford to buy nonessential items.	**Postwar Frame of Mind** Answers will vary. Missourians were happy the fighting was over and tried to move on and put the wars behind them. People were hopeful and went back to work.

MISSOURI
Then and Now
CHAPTER 14: SOME GOOD TIMES AND BAD TIMES

CURRICULUM ALIGNMENT	
THE SHOW-ME STANDARDS:	KNOWLEDGE STANDARDS: SS2, SS5, SS6
	PROCESS STANDARDS: G1.1, 1.6, 1.8, 1.9, 1.10, 3.1, 3.3, 3.5, 4.1
GRADE LEVEL EXPECTATIONS:	SS2, CONCEPT A1; SS3, CONCEPT A1; SS4, CONCEPT D4; SS5, CONCEPT D4; SS6, CONCEPT A1; SS7, CONCEPT A1, B2

CHAPTER 14 ASSESSMENT

Short Answers

1. Great Britain, France, Russia, and some other smaller nations were on one side during World War I. They

   were called the <u>Allies.</u>

2. When the United States joined in the war, it became one of the <u>Allied Powers.</u>

3. World War I lasted from <u>1914</u> to <u>1918.</u>

4. Which side won World War I? the Allies

5. The year 1929 was the beginning of hard times in America, What was this period called?

   the Great Depression

6. What was the name of Charles Lindbergh's plane? the *Spirit of St. Louis*

7. Which famous Missourian was called "Captain Harry" during World War I?

   Harry Truman

8. Name three new weapons that changed the way World War I was fought.

   submarine, machine gun, and poison gas

True or False

9. __F__ During the 1930s, white and black baseball players played on the same teams.

10. __T__ African Americans and women could vote in the 1930s.

11. __T__ Submarines were called U-boats by the Germans.

12. __T__ The national government hired people without jobs during the Great Depression.

13. __F__ During the depression, the May family bought their meat and mushrooms at the grocery store.

135

CHAPTER 14 ASSESSMENT (cont.)

Vocabulary

14. Below is a word used in the chapter. In the spaces provided, write a definition of the word, list a synonym for the word, and draw a picture that illustrates the word's meaning.

depression

Definition: a period of time in which business is slow and many people are out of work

Synonym: some possible answers are *recession, decline, slump*

Illustration: answers will vary

15. Explain how the word relates to the chapter. Answers will vary.

Demonstrating Your Knowledge

16. How might a child of the Great Depression feel about brand name and designer clothing that children wear today? Explain your reasoning.

    Answers will vary.

17. Describe three ways that Missourians helped the war effort during World War I. Are these things that Missourians would do today to help during a war?

    Answers will vary for this two-part question. Some suggested answers for the first part—ways that Missourians helped the war effort—are below.

    - Numerous Missourians joined the army and navy.
    - Women worked as volunteers in Red Cross canteens in Europe.
    - Farmers raised extra food to help feed America.
    - Families did not waste anything.
    - Families raised gardens to provide more food.
    - Missourians ate less sugar and meat.
    - People sent everything they could to Europe to support the war.
    - Workers in factories produced items needed to fight the war.
    - Missourians bought war bonds to help support the war.

CHAPTER 14 ASSESSMENT (cont.)

18. Create a graphic organizer to illustrate the status of the African Americans' fight for equal rights between the wars.

Organizers and information will vary. Some suggested information is below.

- Black Missourians were allowed to vote.
- In 1921 Missouri voters elected the first black member of the Missouri General Assembly.
- Many African American leaders worked to end segregation.
- Missouri was still a segregated state.
- There were separate schools for blacks.
- There were no law schools open to black students.
- African Americans could not stay at most hotels.
- Most restaurants served only whites.
- African American baseball players could not play on white teams.

Answers could also include the accomplishments of the following African Americans:

- Homer G. Phillips
- Lloyd Gaines
- Lucile Bluford

MISSOURI
Then and Now
CHAPTER 15: MISSOURIANS JOIN STRUGGLES

CURRICULUM ALIGNMENT

THE SHOW-ME STANDARDS: KNOWLEDGE STANDARDS: SS2, SS6
PROCESS STANDARDS: G1.8
GRADE LEVEL EXPECTATIONS: SS5, CONCEPT D4

VOCABULARY INSIGHTS

1. dictator

a. Definition: a ruler who has complete control over a country and its people

b. Write a sentence from the chapter using the word:
Page 303: Leaders called **dictators** took over governments in Germany, Italy, and Japan.
These **dictators** wanted to control everything.
The **dictators** built large armies.
Adolf Hitler was the German **dictator**.

c. Create your own sentence: answers will vary

d. Illustrate the word: answers will vary

2. barracks

a. Definition: buildings in which soldiers live

b. Write a sentence from the chapter using the word:
Page 306: Some soldiers also trained at Jefferson **Barracks** near St. Louis.

c. Create your own sentence: answers will vary

d. Illustrate the word: answers will vary

VOCABULARY INSIGHTS (cont.)

3. peace

    a. Definition: the absence of war; quiet; stillness

    b. Write a sentence from the chapter using the word:
        Page 303: Leaders from different countries had worked to bring **peace** to the world.
                But the **peace** did not last long.
        Page 309: Since World War II it has sent troops to many parts of the world to help keep the **peace**.
        Page 316: He helped the world to make the change from a time of war to a time of **peace**.

    c. Create your own sentence: answers will vary

    d. Illustrate the word: answers will vary

4. recycle

    a. Definition: to process something so that it can be used again

    b. Write a sentence from the chapter using the word:
        Page 306: These products were **recycled** and used to make things needed to fight the war.

    c. Create your own sentence: answers will vary

    d. Illustrate the word: answers will vary

CURRICULUM ALIGNMENT

THE SHOW-ME STANDARDS: KNOWLEDGE STANDARDS: SS2, SS5, SS6

PROCESS STANDARDS: G1.2, 1.6, 1.8

GRADE LEVEL EXPECTATIONS: SS2, CONCEPT A1, B2, C3

SS7, CONCEPT A1

HOW WORLD WAR II BEGAN

Fill in the chart to show the chain of events that led the U.S. to declare war on the Axis Powers.

THE BEGINNING

Dictators take over governments in Germany, Italy, and Japan, which become the Axis Powers. The dictators build large armies and use them to take over other countries.

Hitler sends his armies into nearby countries. England and France try to stop him and declare war on Germany. Russia agrees to fight with England and France against the Axis countries. England, France, and Russia call themselves the Allies.

The United States wants the Allies to win, but wants to stay out of the war. It sends ships and guns to the Allies to help them defeat Hitler.

Japanese airplanes drop bombs on the United States military base at Pearl Harbor in Hawaii.

The United States Congress declares war on Japan and the other Axis countries.

CURRICULUM ALIGNMENT

THE SHOW-ME STANDARDS:	KNOWLEDGE STANDARDS: SS2, SS6
	PROCESS STANDARDS: G1.1, 1.6, 1.8, 1.9
GRADE LEVEL EXPECTATIONS:	SS2, CONCEPT A1, B2, C3
	SS7, CONCEPT B2

PATRIOTIC MISSOURIANS

Just as they did in World War I, Missourians stepped up and did their part to help in the war effort during World War II. Create a graphic organizer below to compare and contrast the ways in which Missourians helped the war effort during the two world wars.

Organizers and information will vary. Teachers may use the Diagram Scoring Guide to score this activity. Some pertinent information is below:

World War I

- Women worked as volunteers in Red Cross canteens in Europe.
- Families raised gardens to provide more food.
- Missourians ate less sugar and meat.
- Missourians sent everything they could to Europe to support the war.

Similarities:
- Many Missourians joined the army and navy.
- Farmers raised extra food to help feed America.
- Families did not waste anything.
- Workers in factories produced items needed to fight the war.
- Missourians bought war bonds to help support the war.

World War II

- Some city boys and girls spent summers on farms to help with the farm work.
- Missouri's minerals were used to make weapons.
- Automobile factories stopped making cars and started making airplanes and tanks.
- Women began working in the factories as the men went off to war.

Similarities:
- Numerous Missourians served in the armed forces.
- Farmers produced extra corn, wheat, oats, cotton, soybeans, and livestock.
- Workers in factories made airplanes, tanks, guns, bullets, chemicals, trucks, machinery, and medical supplies. They also made uniforms and shoes for people in the armed forces.
- Missourians bought war bonds to help pay for the war.
- People tried not to waste anything. Children collected grease, newspapers, and scrap metal to be recycled to make things needed to fight the war.

CURRICULUM ALIGNMENT

THE SHOW-ME STANDARDS: KNOWLEDGE STANDARDS: SS2, SS6
                                               PROCESS STANDARDS: G1.1, 1.2, 1.6, 1.8, 1.10

GRADE LEVEL EXPECTATIONS: SS2, CONCEPT A1, B2, C3
                                              SS7, CONCEPT A1

TIMELINE

Choose five events from Chapter 15 and create a timeline. Write an appropriate title for your timeline in the box provided below.

Answers will vary. Teachers may use the Diagram Scoring Guide to score this activity.

Timeline Title

CURRICULUM ALIGNMENT	
THE SHOW-ME STANDARDS:	KNOWLEDGE STANDARDS: SS2, SS6
	PROCESS STANDARDS: G1.8, 1.10, 2.5, 3.3, 3.4, 3.6
GRADE LEVEL EXPECTATIONS:	SS2, CONCEPT A1; SS3, CONCEPT A1; SS6, CONCEPT C3; SS7, CONCEPT B2

ORDINARY CITIZENS

Ordinary people can accomplish great things. Some examples are Ivory Perry, Captain Wendell Pruitt, and Lucile H. Bluford. Think about your school or neighborhood. Are there conditions or problems that you would like to change to make your world a better place? How can you go about creating change in a positive way? Identify a problem and a plan of action, and illustrate them in the circle below.

Problem: Answers will vary.

Plan of Action: Answers will vary.

CURRICULUM ALIGNMENT
THE SHOW-ME STANDARDS: KNOWLEDGE STANDARDS: SS1, SS2,
                           SS5, SS6
                           PROCESS STANDARDS: G1.1, 1.6, 1.8, 1.10,
                           2.5, 3.5, 3.6, 4.1, 4.2
GRADE LEVEL EXPECTATIONS: SS2, CONCEPT A1, B2, C3;
                           SS3, CONCEPT A1;
                           SS6, CONCEPT C3; SS7, CONCEPT A1

CHAPTER 15 ASSESSMENT

Vocabulary

1. Below is a word used in the chapter. In the spaces provided, write a definition of the word, list a synonym for the word, and draw a picture that illustrates the word's meaning.

dictator

Definition: a ruler who has complete control over a country and its people

Synonym: some possible answers are *tyrant, oppressor, bully*

Illustration: answers will vary

2. Explain how the word relates to the chapter. Answers will vary.

Short Answers

3. List four characteristics that made Harry S. Truman a remarkable man and a great president.

    Answers will vary. Following are some suggested characteristics:
    He was a good leader, popular with his men, honest, a hard worker, could take charge of situations, tried to make things better for the American people, started many programs to help other countries that had been destroyed by war, knew how to talk to people, and was a good listener.

4. Which of the two powers fighting in World War II did not believe in democracy? Give an example of this side's undemocratic behavior.

    The Axis Powers—Germany, Italy, and Japan—did not believe in democracy. Examples will vary; suggested points follow: Dictators took over governments in Germany, Italy, and Japan. They wanted to control everything. The people in those countries had very little freedom. The dictators built large armies and used them to take over other countries. Adolf Hitler was a German dictator who ordered the killing of many Jews, which was called the Holocaust.

5. The United States did not want to get involved in World War II. What was the last straw that forced the country to declare war?

    the bombing of the U.S. military base at Pearl Harbor, Hawaii, by Japan

6. What circumstances caused Truman to become president?

    Truman was vice president to President Franklin D. Roosevelt. When Roosevelt died suddenly, Truman became president.

CHAPTER 15 ASSESSMENT (cont.)

7.   Explain the reason for the Civil Rights movement.

It had been almost 100 years since the Civil War had ended slavery in the United States. But Missouri was still a segregated state, as was much of the country. African Americans had fought alongside whites to defend their country, yet they did not have the same rights. They could vote, but they still had to attend all-black schools that were not as good as white schools. African Americans were not welcome at many restaurants, hotels, theaters, parks, and other places. They could not get good jobs because many employers would not hire them. African Americans decided this all had to change, and they worked to put an end to segregation. Many white people also felt that segregation was unfair and wrong, and they worked to help African Americans gain equal rights. The resulting Civil Rights movement helped pass laws to give the same rights to all Americans.

Using Inference Skills

8.   The United States was founded on the concept of democracy, yet African Americans and women fought for equal rights for many decades. Why do you think it took so long for these two groups to attain equal rights?

Answers will vary. Teachers may use the Writing Scoring Guide to score questions 8 and 9.

9.   Several people in this chapter worked to improve humankind and made the world a better place through their efforts. Think about the lives of these people and, in paragraph form, describe the qualities you believe ordinary people must possess in order to be able to make positive changes in the world.

Answers will vary.

CHAPTER 15 ASSESSMENT (cont.)

10. Missourians are patriotic and loyal people. Compare and contrast the ways they helped their country through two wars.

Answers will vary. Teachers may use the Diagram Scoring Guide to score this question. Main points are below.

COMPARING MISSOURIANS' WAR EFFORTS

World War I
Women worked as volunteers in Red Cross canteens in Europe. Families raised gardens to provide more food. Missourians ate less sugar and meat. They sent everything they could to Europe to support the war.

World War II
Some city boys and girls spent summers on farms to help with farm work. Missouri's minerals were used to make weapons. Automobile factories stopped making cars and started making airplanes and tanks. Women began working in the factories as the men went off to war.

Similarities
Many Missourians served in the armed forces. Farmers raised extra food to help feed America. Families did not waste anything. Workers in factories produced items needed to fight the war. Missourians bought war bonds to help support the war.

CURRICULUM ALIGNMENT
THE SHOW-ME STANDARDS: KNOWLEDGE STANDARDS: SS2, SS6
                          PROCESS STANDARDS: G1.8
GRADE LEVEL EXPECTATIONS: SS5, CONCEPT D4

VOCABULARY INSIGHTS

1. county

    a. Definition: a division of a state or nation for local government

    b. Write a sentence from the chapter using the word:
       Page 332: Missouri is divided into 114 **counties**, plus the city of St. Louis, which is considered the same as a **county**.
           It is separate from St. Louis **County**.
           Some of the most important **county** leaders are the **county** commissioners, the sheriff, and the tax
              collector.
           The **county** governments provide for people who live outside the cities many of the same things that
              cities do for their residents.
           There are several school districts in each **county**.

    c. Create your own sentence: answers will vary

    d. Illustrate the word: answers will vary

2. income tax

    a. Definition: a tax on money earned by people or companies

    b. Write a sentence from the chapter using the words:
       Page 333: Another tax is the **income tax**.
             The more money a person earns, the more **income tax** the person usually pays.

    c. Create your own sentence: answers will vary

    d. Illustrate the word: answers will vary

VOCABULARY INSIGHTS (cont.)

3. jury

    a. Definition: a group of persons selected to hear evidence in a law court and give a decision on that evidence

    b. Write a sentence from the chapter using the word:
        Page 331: When a person is accused of breaking a law, the person is usually brought before a judge and a **jury** for a trial.
               A **jury** is a group of citizens.
               The **jury** and the judge decide whether or not the person has broken the law.

    c. Create your own sentence: answers will vary

    d. Illustrate the word: answers will vary

4. mayor

    a. Definition: a person chosen to be the main leader of a city or town

    b. Write a sentence from the chapter using the word:
        Page 332: Most cities have a **mayor**.
               The **mayor** carries out the laws.

    c. Create your own sentence: answers will vary

    d. Illustrate the word: answers will vary

CURRICULUM ALIGNMENT
THE SHOW-ME STANDARDS: KNOWLEDGE STANDARDS: SS1, SS3, SS6
PROCESS STANDARDS: G1.2, 1.6, 1.8, 4.2, 4.3
GRADE LEVEL EXPECTATIONS: SS3, CONCEPT B2, C3
SS7, CONCEPT A1

STATE GOVERNMENT

Label the Missouri government chart correctly and explain the job of each branch.

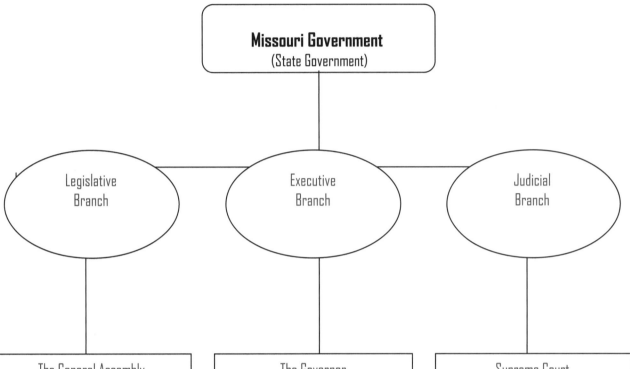

The General Assembly

This branch makes the laws for the state. The people elect the members of the General Assembly.
The two parts of the General Assembly are the State House of Representatives and the State Senate.

The Governor

This branch enforces the laws. The governor is the main officer of this branch of government. The people elect the governor. The governor makes sure that the laws are carried out. There are many departments that help the governor do his or her job. One is the department of transportation. It helps build and take care of roads in Missouri. Another department is the department of elementary and secondary education. It helps run Missouri's public schools.

Supreme Court

This branch helps settle disputes and interprets what the law means. Disagreements between people are settled in a court. When a person is accused of breaking the law, he or she is usually brought before a judge and a jury for a trial. The jury and judge decide whether or not the person has broken the law.

MISSOURI
Then and Now
CHAPTER 16: GOVERNMENT IN MISSOURI

CURRICULUM ALIGNMENT

THE SHOW-ME STANDARDS: KNOWLEDGE STANDARDS: SS1, SS3, SS6
                        PROCESS STANDARDS: G1.2, 1.6, 1.8,
                        4.2, 4.3
GRADE LEVEL EXPECTATIONS: SS3, CONCEPT B2, C3
                          SS7, CONCEPT A1

NATIONAL GOVERNMENT

Label the U.S. government chart correctly and explain the job of each branch.

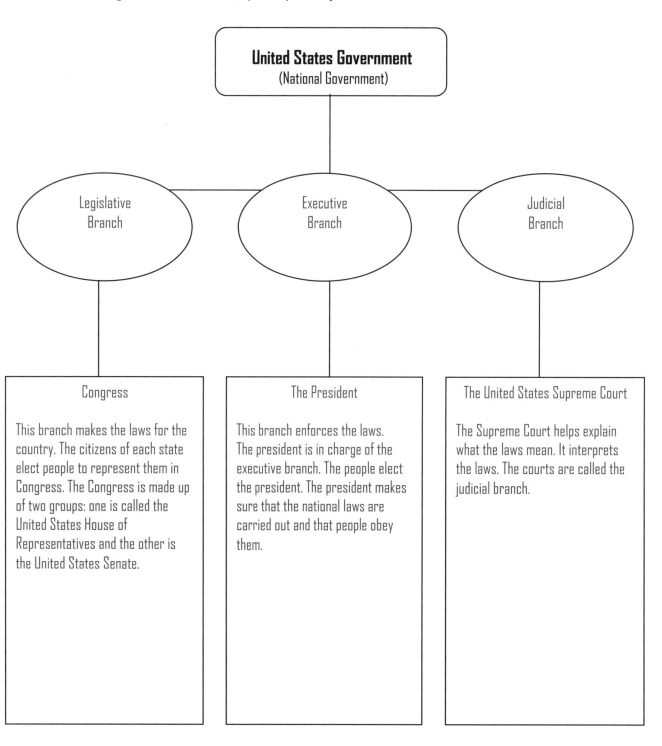

United States Government
(National Government)

Legislative Branch

Executive Branch

Judicial Branch

Congress

This branch makes the laws for the country. The citizens of each state elect people to represent them in Congress. The Congress is made up of two groups: one is called the United States House of Representatives and the other is the United States Senate.

The President

This branch enforces the laws. The president is in charge of the executive branch. The people elect the president. The president makes sure that the national laws are carried out and that people obey them.

The United States Supreme Court

The Supreme Court helps explain what the laws mean. It interprets the laws. The courts are called the judicial branch.

150

CURRICULUM ALIGNMENT
THE SHOW-ME STANDARDS: KNOWLEDGE STANDARDS: SS1, SS3, SS6
                                              PROCESS STANDARDS: G1.2, 1.6, 1.8, 4.2, 4.3
GRADE LEVEL EXPECTATIONS: SS3, CONCEPT B2, C3
                                              SS7, CONCEPT A1

COMPARING STATE AND NATIONAL GOVERNMENTS

Use the diagram below to compare and contrast the state government and national government.

Answers will vary. Suggested answers are below. Teachers may use the Diagram Scoring Guide to score this activity.

State Government

States have a constitution. The state government is divided into three branches: the legislative branch, the executive branch, and the judicial branch.

- The legislative branch contains the General Assembly. The two parts of the General Assembly are the State House of Representatives and the State Senate.
- The executive branch houses the Governor.
- The judicial branch contains the Supreme Court.

State governments operate schools. They build roads and bridges. They pass laws to protect lives and property.

Government of the United States

The United States government is divided into three branches. They are the executive, legislative, and judicial branches.

- The President is in charge of the executive branch. The President enforces the laws.
- The legislative branch houses the Congress. The Congress is made up of two groups: the United States House of Representatives and the United States Senate.
- The judicial branch contains the United States Supreme Court.

The national government runs the armed forces to protect us from foreign enemies, makes treaties with other countries, prints our paper money and makes our coins, helps take care of old and needy people, operates national parks, and runs a postal service to deliver mail.

Similarities

They both have a constitution. They have the same three branches of government. The General Assemblies have representatives and senates.

CURRICULUM ALIGNMENT
THE SHOW-ME STANDARDS: KNOWLEDGE STANDARDS: SS1, SS3, SS6
PROCESS STANDARDS: G1.2, 1.6, 1.8, 3.1,
4.2, 4.3
GRADE LEVEL EXPECTATIONS: SS1, CONCEPT A1
SS7, CONCEPT A1

THE IMPORTANCE OF LAWS

Governments were set up to make laws and to make sure that everyone follows them. Laws are like rules. Can you imagine what our society would be like without laws to protect us?

On the left side of the chart, list four laws that we have to follow as citizens. On the right, explain what would happen if we didn't have those laws.

Four laws:	Consequences of not having laws:
Answers will vary.	Students should note reasonable consequences of not having the laws they have chosen.

CURRICULUM ALIGNMENT
THE SHOW-ME STANDARDS: KNOWLEDGE STANDARDS: SS1, SS3, SS6
                            PROCESS STANDARDS: G1.2, 1.8, 3.1, 4.2, 4.3
GRADE LEVEL EXPECTATIONS: SS1, CONCEPT B2

RESPONSIBILITIES OF GOOD CITIZENS

A democracy is a government run by the people. Citizens of a democracy have certain responsibilities. In the boxes below, list the five main responsibilities that citizens must assume in order for democracy to work well.

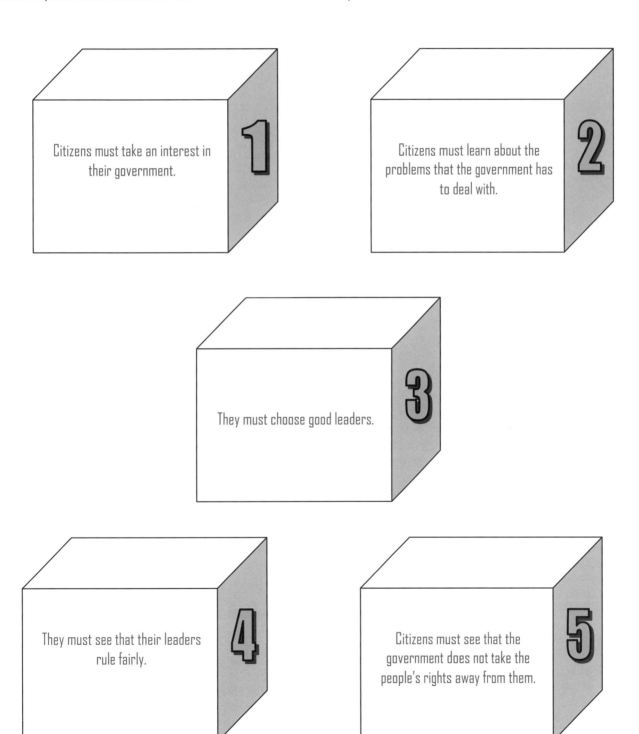

Citizens must take an interest in their government.
1

Citizens must learn about the problems that the government has to deal with.
2

They must choose good leaders.
3

They must see that their leaders rule fairly.
4

Citizens must see that the government does not take the people's rights away from them.
5

CURRICULUM ALIGNMENT

THE SHOW-ME STANDARDS: KNOWLEDGE STANDARDS: SS1, SS2, SS3, SS5, SS6
PROCESS STANDARDS: G1.1, 1.6, 1.8, 1.10, 2.5, 3.5, 3.6, 4.1, 4.2
GRADE LEVEL EXPECTATIONS: SS1, CONCEPT A1, B2; SS3, CONCEPT B2, C3; SS4, CONCEPT C3; SS5, CONCEPT D4; SS7, CONCEPT B2

CHAPTER 16 ASSESSMENT

True or False

1. __F__ The president makes the laws.

2. __T__ The government gets money from the people.

3. __T__ The General Assembly makes laws for the state.

4. __T__ The Bill of Rights protects our freedom of speech.

5. __F__ The Supreme Court is in the legislative branch.

6. __T__ Today some countries are run by dictators.

7. __T__ In a democracy, people elect their leaders.

8. __T__ Citizens of a democracy have responsibilities.

9. __F__ The mayor is the leader of the county.

10. __F__ The sheriff works for the city.

Short Answers

11. What type of tax is added to the price of things you buy? sales tax

12. What type of tax is based on the money you earn? income tax

13. What type of tax provides schools, libraries, cities, and counties with money? property tax

14. The group of people who run a city is the city council.

15. Why do we have governments? Governments were set up to make rules and to make sure that everyone follows the rules. These rules are known as laws. People need laws and rules to prevent conflicts and to provide for the safety, welfare, and rights of everyone. Governments also provide many services for people.

16. What are the three branches of the state government? legislative, executive, and judicial

17. Why do the people of a democratic government elect leaders? A democracy is a government run by the people. The people have the right to vote to choose their leader and to voice their opinion.

CHAPTER 16 ASSESSMENT (cont.)

Demonstrating Your Knowledge

18. a) Explain why laws or rules are important.
    b) Create a rule that would be valuable to your classroom or school, and explain why it is needed.

    a) Laws and rules help prevent conflicts between people. They also provide safety and welfare and protect people's rights. Without rules, people would do whatever they wanted to do. They might choose to do things that would hurt other people. They might not respect the rights of others. We have rules to keep that from happening.

    b) Answers will vary.

19. a) Explain the term *democracy* and the responsibilities of citizens in a democracy.
    b) Name one responsibility you have as a member of your classroom, and explain why it is important.

    a) A democracy is a government run by the people. People have rights and more freedom in a democratic government. They have the right to hold elections and to choose leaders.

    The responsibilities of citizens are:
    - to take an interest in their government.
    - to learn about the problems that the government has to deal with.
    - to choose good leaders.
    - to see that their leaders rule fairly.
    - to see that the government does not take the people's rights away from them.

    b) Answers will vary.

20. Explain how the government gets money in order to run our country.

    The government gets money mainly from taxes. Each citizen must pay taxes. There are several kinds of taxes. A sales tax is added to the price of things you buy; the store sends the tax money to the government. Another tax is income tax. The more money a person earns, the more income tax he or she usually pays. The property tax provides schools, libraries, cities, and counties with some of their money. There are many other taxes, such as gasoline and cigarette taxes.

CHAPTER 16 ASSESSMENT (cont.)

Vocabulary

21. Below is a word used in the chapter. In the spaces provided, write a definition of the word, list a synonym for the word, and draw a picture that illustrates the word's meaning.

jury

Definition: a group of persons selected to hear evidence in a law court and give a decision on that evidence

Synonym: some possible answers are *judges, panel, ruling body*

Illustration: answers will vary

22. Explain how the word relates to the chapter. Answers will vary.

Government Diagram

23. Draw a diagram comparing the state and national governments. Describe each branch, its responsibilities, and its leader.

Answers will vary. Teachers may adapt the Diagram Scoring Guide to evaluate this answer. Suggested answer content is below.

State Government

The Legislative Branch: the General Assembly
This branch makes the laws for the state. The people elect the members of the General Assembly.
The two parts of the General Assembly are the State House of Representatives and the State Senate.

The Executive Branch: the Governor
This branch enforces the laws. The governor is the main officer of this branch of government. The people elect the governor. The governor makes sure that the laws are carried out. There are many departments that help the governor do this job. One is the department of transportation. It helps build and take care of roads in Missouri. Another is the department of elementary and secondary education, which helps run Missouri's public schools.

The Judicial Branch: the Supreme Court
This branch helps settle disputes and interprets what the law means. Disagreements between people are settled in a court. When a person is accused of breaking the law, he or she is usually brought before a judge and a jury for a trial. The jury and judge decide whether or not the person has broken the law.

CHAPTER 16 ASSESSMENT (cont.)

(question 23, cont.)

National Government

The Legislative Branch: Congress
This branch makes the laws for the country. The citizens of each state elect people to represent them in Congress. The Congress is made up of two groups: the United States House of Representatives and the United States Senate.

The Executive Branch: the President
This branch enforces the laws. The president is in charge of the executive branch. The people elect the president. The president makes sure that the national laws are carried out and that people obey them.

The Judicial Branch: the United States Supreme Court
The Supreme Court helps explain what the laws mean. It interprets the laws. The courts are called the judicial branch.

MISSOURI
Then and Now
CHAPTER 17: MISSOURI AT THE START . . .

VOCABULARY INSIGHTS

1. erosion

    a. Definition: the wearing away of something, such as land, by the action of water or wind

    b. Write a sentence from the chapter using the word:
       Page 341: Many Missouri farmers work hard to prevent wind and water **erosion**.
       Page 348: This caused soil **erosion**.

    c. Create your own sentence: answers will vary

    d. Illustrate the word: answers will vary

2. manufacturing

    a. Definition: the making of products by hand or machine

    b. Write a sentence from the chapter using the word:
       Page 342: St. Louis is still the state's most important **manufacturing** center.
                 Kansas City has many **manufacturing** plants.
                 Manufacturing is changing.

    c. Create your own sentence: answers will vary

    d. Illustrate the word: answers will vary

VOCABULARY INSIGHTS (cont.)

3. interstate

    a. Definition: between states

    b. Write a sentence from the chapter using the word:
        Page 349: Missourians can travel in their motor vehicles along **interstate** highways and modern hard-surface roads to all parts of the state.

    c. Create your own sentence: answers will vary

    d. Illustrate the word: answers will vary

4. tourist

    a. Definition: a person who is traveling for fun and recreation

    b. Write a sentence from the chapter using the word:
        Page 344: The **tourist** industry is big business in Missouri today.
                The Ozarks are especially popular with **tourists**.
                This small Ozarks town has become one of the most popular **tourist** spots in the United States.
                Another of the state's top **tourist** attractions is located in nearby Springfield.
                Many **tourists** who visit Springfield also go to the Wilson's Creek National Battlefield.
        Page 345: Missouri's largest cities, St. Louis and Kansas City, attract crowds of **tourists** looking for fun, recreation, entertainment, and opportunities to see and learn about new things.
                In nearby Independence, the Truman Library and the National Frontier Trails Center are popular **tourist** attractions.

    c. Create your own sentence: answers will vary

    d. Illustrate the word: answers will vary

CURRICULUM ALIGNMENT
THE SHOW-ME STANDARDS: KNOWLEDGE STANDARDS: SS2, SS5, SS6
PROCESS STANDARDS: G1.2, 1.6, 1.8, 1.9, 3.5
GRADE LEVEL EXPECTATIONS: SS2, CONCEPT A1
SS5, CONCEPT G7

MISSOURI'S FARMING HISTORY

Why do farmers today produce more food than previous generations of farmers? The modern machinery and computers that farmers use today can do the work of many people.

In the spaces below, list the different ways that each group of Missourians farmed the land.

Pioneer Farmers	Pioneer farmers tried to find land with timber because they believed that land that could grow trees would be good for growing crops. They had to clear the land for their crops; for the first few years they planted seeds around tree stumps and roots. The ground was tough, and they used wooden plows to break the earth. Most farmers raised corn. It grew well and they could use it to make corn bread, hominy, and whiskey. It could also be stored and fed to their animals. Farmers used oxen and horses for plowing and transportation. Cows supplied butter and milk. The cattle and hogs often ran wild in the woods. Frontier farms had to produce almost everything the pioneer family needed, and they had to grow enough food for winter. Fruits and vegetables were dried, and meat was cured with salt. Pioneers hunted deer, bear, turkey, and other wild game. They also fished. They made their own maple sugar and salt. All family members worked on the farm.
Post-Civil War Farmers	Many new farms were started after the Civil War. Farmers began using more machines, such as corn planters, binders, threshing machines, hay balers, corn shellers, and plows with wheels and a seat for the driver. Horses or mules pulled most of these new machines; a few were run by steam engines. Missouri farmers began looking for new fertilizers and better kinds of seeds. Scientists at the University of Missouri, founded in 1870, helped farmers find better ways to farm. Missouri's most important crops were corn, wheat, barley, tobacco, hay, fruit, and vegetables. Farmers also raised cattle, hogs, horses, mules, sheep, and chickens.
21st Century Farmers	There are fewer farmers today but they grow more food. Farms are larger and most farmers use modern farm equipment. More farmers are using computers to help them keep records and operate machinery. The modern machinery and computers can do the work of many people. Farmers plow fertilizer into the soil to make the plants produce more. Many farmers use chemicals to kill weeds and insects. Farmers must know how to use chemicals properly in order to protect the environment from pollution. Organic farmers do not use chemicals, but instead grow food the old way. Today's farmers also practice conservation and work to prevent wind and water erosion.

MISSOURI
Then and Now
CHAPTER 17: MISSOURI AT THE START . . .

CURRICULUM ALIGNMENT

THE SHOW-ME STANDARDS: KNOWLEDGE STANDARDS: SS2, SS5, SS6
                         PROCESS STANDARDS: G1.1, 1.2, 1.8, 4.1
GRADE LEVEL EXPECTATIONS: SS2, CONCEPT A1;
                         SS5, CONCEPT D4, E5; SS7, CONCEPT A1

MISSOURI TRANSPORTATION

Missourians have always been on the move. Through the years they have continued to improve upon methods of transportation.

1. How many methods of transportation can you recall from Missouri's history? Write them down and state which one you think has had the biggest impact on Missourians.

    Answers will vary. Suggested answers are canoes, dugouts, flatboats, keelboats, steamboats, railroads, cars, airplanes, and space travel.

2. Write a paragraph about why you think the method of transportation you chose was the one that made the biggest impact. Explain your reasoning and identify the information you used to make your decision.

    Answers will vary. Teachers may use the Writing Scoring Guide to score this activity.

CURRICULUM ALIGNMENT

THE SHOW-ME STANDARDS: KNOWLEDGE STANDARDS: SS2, SS5, SS6
                         PROCESS STANDARDS: G1.2, 1.6, 1.8, 1.10,
                         3.5, 4.1
GRADE LEVEL EXPECTATIONS: SS2, CONCEPT A1
                         SS5, CONCEPT E5

TECHNOLOGY IN MISSOURI

List six different ways that you use technology daily.

1. Answers will vary.   4. _____

2. _____   5. _____

3. _____   6. _____

How has the invention of the computer affected our lives? Brainstorm your ideas and write a paragraph below explaining how computers have affected the lives of Missourians.

Answers will vary. Teachers may use the Writing Scoring Guide to score this activity.

SHOW-ME BROCHURE

Using the template below or a sheet of white paper folded into thirds, research a location in Missouri and design a brochure that will encourage people to visit. Compile some facts and use your creativity to help promote the location.

Answers will vary. Teachers may use the Brochure Scoring Guide to score this activity.

CURRICULUM ALIGNMENT
THE SHOW-ME STANDARDS: KNOWLEDGE STANDARDS: SS2, SS4, SS5,
                          SS6
                          PROCESS STANDARDS: G1.6, 1.8,1.9, 3.1,
                          3.5,4.1
GRADE LEVEL EXPECTATIONS: SS2, CONCEPT A1
                           SS5, CONCEPT D4, E5; SS7, CONCEPT A1, B2

CHAPTER 17 ASSESSMENT

Vocabulary

1. Below is a word used in the chapter. In the spaces provided, write a definition of the word, list a synonym for the word, and draw a picture that illustrates the word's meaning.

tourist

Definition: a person who is traveling for fun and recreation

Synonym: some possible answers are *traveler, wanderer, pilgrim*

Illustration: answers will vary

2. Explain how the word relates to the chapter. Answers will vary.

Short Answers

3. Missouri has always been a rich land, and many people over the years have enjoyed the state's natural resources. What could happen to our natural resources if they are not protected?

    They could be destroyed. Trees and forests could be cut down and cause soil erosion, which could eliminate cover for wildlife. Wild game could become scarce. The rivers and lakes could be polluted, causing fish to die.

4. What was the purpose of the first computers, and when were they built?

    Scientists and engineers built the first computers during World War II. They used them to develop new weapons. Computers made it possible to store and sort large amounts of information.

5. Why is this called the information age?

    In the 1980s personal computers became available to families, schools, offices and small businesses. Later, PCs were connected to form the Internet and the World Wide Web. This allowed anyone with a computer to get all kinds of information very quickly. Also, computers make it possible to store and sort large amounts of information.

6. Why is more food grown and more products manufactured today despite the fact that there are fewer farmers and factory workers?

    Farms are larger and farmers use modern farm machinery and computers that make keeping records and operating machinery easier to do. Computers control much of factory production and robots have replaced many workers on the assembly line.

CHAPTER 17 ASSESSMENT (cont.)

Using Inference Skills

7. Explain the difference between providing a service and providing a product. Give an example of each.

    Answers will vary, but in broad terms, providing a service is doing work for others as part of an occupation or business, and providing a product is offering merchandise for sale. Examples will vary.

8. Missourians Sam Walton and J. C. Penney discovered profitable ways to sell products and became successful businessmen. Explain some things that you would do as a businessperson to increase your business and to bring customers to your products.

    Answers will vary. Some possible answers are:
    - Place your business in a location where there are many people, such as a mall or shopping center
    - Put your business on the Internet for E-business.
    - Create a chain of stores and place them in small towns.
    - Buy large amounts of merchandise at cheap prices and sell them at bargain prices.

9. Missouri has many tourist attractions. Explain how the tourist industry maintains its status as big business and helps Missouri grow.

    Answers will vary. Millions of people come to see tourist attractions. In addition to spending money on these attractions, in they spend at motels, restaurants, and in surrounding towns. The towns and the state benefit from this money and it helps their communities.

10. The Mississippi and Missouri Rivers have always been important to Missourians. Explain the history of the rivers' importance, concluding with their importance today. You may include diagrams or illustrations in your response.

    Answers will vary. Teachers may use the Writing and Diagram Scoring Guides to score this question.

    Main points:
    The rivers were the first highways. The Indians and European explorers and pioneer settlers traveled the rivers when they could because it was faster than traveling over land. The early settlers used the rivers to transport their goods and produce on flatboats, keelboats, and then steamboats to many parts of the country. River travel made trading with other places easier. Early towns were built around the rivers. The rivers are still major transportation routes. Barges use the rivers today to transport grain and other bulky products to many parts of the United States.

VOCABULARY INSIGHTS

1. composer

   a. Definition: a person who writes music

   b. Write a sentence from the chapter using the word:
      Page 365: They liked to perform pieces written by famous **composers**.
               W. C. Handy, Scott Joplin, Charlie "Bird" Parker, and William "Count" Basie were all famous African
                  American **composers** and musicians.
      Page 367: Joplin began **composing** his own tunes.
               The people of Sedalia hold a music festival to honor this famous American **composer**.

   c. Create your own sentence: answers will vary

   d. Illustrate the word: answers will vary

2. cartoon

   a. Definition: an amusing sketch

   b. Write a sentence from the chapter using the word:
      Page 363: Disney created Mickey Mouse, Donald Duck, and many other **cartoon** characters.
               Disney began drawing **cartoons**, but his **cartoons** were different.
               He made his first moving **cartoon** films in Kansas City.
               There he made short **cartoon** movies.
      Page 364: Walt Disney's most famous **cartoon** characters are Mickey Mouse and Donald Duck.
      Page 365: One day while riding on a train, Disney got the idea to make a **cartoon** about a mouse.
               But Walt Disney was always looking for ways to improve his **cartoons**.
               Mickey Mouse was a character in Disney's first **cartoon** movie that used sound.
               Walt Disney's **cartoons** made him famous all over the world.

   c. Create your own sentence: answers will vary

   d. Illustrate the word: answers will vary

VOCABULARY INSIGHTS (cont.)

3. mural

    a. Definition: a picture, usually of great size, painted on a wall

    b. Write a sentence from the chapter using the word:
        Page 362: Benton painted many **murals**.
                Some of his most famous **murals** are in Missouri.
                He painted a **mural** in the state capitol building in Jefferson City.
                Benton liked to include all kinds of people in his **murals**.
                Another of Benton's **murals** is in the Truman Library in Independence.
        Page 363: Thomas Hart Benton's **mural** in the state capitol building shows life in Missouri.

    c. Create your own sentence: answers will vary

    d. Illustrate the word: answers will vary

4. musician

    a. Definition: a person who writes, sings, or plays music skillfully

    b. Write a sentence from the chapter using the word:
        Page 358: Many fine writers, artists, and **musicians** have come from Missouri.
        Page 365: W. C. Handy, Scott Joplin, Charlie "Bird" Parker, and William "Count" Basie were all famous African
                    American composers and **musicians**.
        Page 366: William "Count" Basie was a famous American jazz **musician**.
                Charles "Bird" Parker was another famous jazz **musician** from Kansas City.
                He played in a band with other black **musicians**.

    c. Create your own sentence: answers will vary

    d. Illustrate the word: answers will vary

CURRICULUM ALIGNMENT
THE SHOW-ME STANDARDS: KNOWLEDGE STANDARDS: SS2, SS5, SS6,
                         FA3, FA5
                         PROCESS STANDARDS: G1.5, 1.6, 1.9, 2.4, 2.5,4.1
GRADE LEVEL EXPECTATIONS: SS2, CONCEPT A1
                         SS7, CONCEPT B2

THOMAS HART BENTON

Thomas Hart Benton, the great-nephew of the Missouri senator of the same name, was a Missouri artist who specialized in painting murals. Much like George Caleb Bingham, he painted things that were happening around him. On page 362 of your textbook is a small part of a mural he painted in the state capitol building.

1.   Do you think that artists can express emotion or feeling in a piece of art? Explain.

      Answers will vary.

2.   Think about something that is important to you—a person, a problem, or issue that you feel strongly about. Draw a picture to illustrate those feelings. Use expression and body language in your illustration to get your idea across.

      Illustrations will vary. Teachers may adapt one of the scoring guides to score this activity.

CURRICULUM ALIGNMENT
THE SHOW-ME STANDARDS: KNOWLEDGE STANDARDS: CA2, SS6, FA3
                                                  PROCESS STANDARDS: G1.5, 1.6, 1.9, 2.4, 2.5, 4.1
GRADE LEVEL EXPECTATIONS: SS2, CONCEPT A1

LANGSTON HUGHES

Before answering the questions below, read Langston Hughes's poem "Dreams," on page 371 of your textbook.

1. What do you think Hughes meant when he wrote: "Life is a broken-winged bird / That cannot fly"?

   Answer will vary. One answer could be that people need dreams to live happily.

2. "Hold fast to dreams" means <u>cherish your dreams, or keep dreaming.</u>

3. What frame of mind do you think Hughes was in when he wrote the lines "For when dreams go / Life is a barren field / Frozen with snow"?

   He was probably disappointed and saddened by the loss of a dream.

4. Do you think the author had any experience with broken or lost dreams? Explain your answer.

   Answers will vary.

5. Do you think that dreams were important to the author? Why or why not?

   Answers will vary.

CURRICULUM ALIGNMENT
THE SHOW-ME STANDARDS: KNOWLEDGE STANDARDS: SS5 SS6, FA3
                         PROCESS STANDARDS: G1.2, 1.6, 1.9, 2.4, 4.1
GRADE LEVEL EXPECTATIONS: SS2, CONCEPT A1
                           SS7, CONCEPT A1

COMPARING MISSOURI AUTHORS

Samuel L. Clemens, Langston Hughes, and Laura Ingalls Wilder were all Missouri authors. How did their writing differ? What types of writing did they do? What parts of the state were they from? Answer these questions about each author below.

Answers will vary. Suggested answers are below.

Samuel Clemens

Samuel Clemens was born in Florida, Missouri. He wrote books and stories under the pen name of Mark Twain. His stories are very humorous and teach us about the people around us. He wrote some stories about his childhood in Hannibal, Missouri, and his life as a steamboat pilot.

Laura Ingalls Wilder

Laura Ingalls Wilder wrote stories about her childhood and pioneer life. Wilder grew up in Wisconsin but moved to Mansfield, Missouri, as an adult. Mansfield is in the Ozarks. Her first book was *Little House in the Big Woods.* She wrote seven more books. Her book *Little House on the Prairie* was made into a television series. Today her home is a museum.

Langston Hughes was born in Joplin, Missouri. He was best known as a poet. He wrote about the lives of African Americans and their struggles. His poems celebrate black people's gifts of song, story, and laughter.

What did all three writers have in common?

Besides having lived in Missouri, they all wrote about things they knew best.

Langston Hughes

170

CURRICULUM ALIGNMENT

THE SHOW-ME STANDARDS: KNOWLEDGE STANDARDS: CA1, SS5 SS6
PROCESS STANDARDS: G1.8, 1.10, 2.1
GRADE LEVEL EXPECTATIONS: SS2, CONCEPT A1

FICTIONAL STORY

Fiction is writing about things that did not really happen. Authors often write fiction based on familiar things and places. Samuel Clemens was one example. Use your imagination and write a fictional short story based on a familiar place, person, activity, or thing.

Answers will vary. Teachers may use the Writing Scoring Guide to score this activity.

CURRICULUM ALIGNMENT

THE SHOW-ME STANDARDS: KNOWLEDGE STANDARDS: SS2, SS5, SS6,
                          FA3, FA5
                          PROCESS STANDARDS: G1.5, 1.6, 1.9, 2.4, 2.5, 4.1
GRADE LEVEL EXPECTATIONS: SS2, CONCEPT A1
                           SS7, CONCEPT B2

WALT DISNEY

Walt Disney was a famous cartoonist and animator. His best-known character was Mickey Mouse. Disney always had faith in his ability to draw. Many people think that they do not have this ability. Let's try a little drawing experiment.

On page 364 of your textbook there is a picture of Mickey Mouse. Turn the picture upside down and draw your own upside-down Mickey in the space below. Begin at the top (with Mickey's feet) and just draw **exactly** what you see, line by line. Do not pay attention to anything else but each line. When you are finished, turn both pictures right-side up, and see how closely your drawing of Mickey matches the original.

Did drawing the picture upside down help? Explain why or why not.

Answers will vary. Turning the picture upside down helps fool the eye into looking at lines instead of concentrating on the figure as a whole.

CURRICULUM ALIGNMENT
THE SHOW-ME STANDARDS: KNOWLEDGE STANDARDS: SS2, SS5, SS6, CA1
                          PROCESS STANDARDS: G1.6, 1.8,1.9, 3.1, 3.5, 4.1
GRADE LEVEL EXPECTATIONS: SS2, CONCEPT A1; SS5, CONCEPT D4;
                          SS7, CONCEPT B2

CHAPTER 18 ASSESSMENT

Short Answers

1. Define the term *fiction*. Fiction is a story made up by a writer. It is something that is not true.

2. Define the term *ballad*. A ballad is a simple song or poem that tells a story.

3. Who was the "King of Ragtime"? Scott Joplin

4. Who wrote *Little House on the Prairie*? Laura Ingalls Wilder

5. Who created Donald Duck? Walt Disney

6. Which artist painted a mural depicting the westward expansion at the Truman Library in Independence, Missouri?

    Thomas Hart Benton

7. Which Missouri-born author wrote about the African American's struggle to gain respect and honor?

    Langston Hughes

True or False

8. __T__ Eugene Field wrote poems for children.

9. __F__ Laura Ingalls Wilder never lived in Missouri.

10. __T__ Blues, ragtime, and jazz are types of music that are important to Missouri history.

11. __F__ The father of the blues was Langston Hughes.

12. __F__ Walt Disney's first full-length movie was *Cinderella*.

13. __F__ Fiction is the kind of writing that is always true.

14. __T__ Samuel Clemens and Langston Hughes both wrote about the things they knew best.

CHAPTER 18 ASSESSMENT (cont.)

Vocabulary

15. Below is a word used in the chapter. In the spaces provided, write a definition of the word, list a synonym for the word, and draw a picture that illustrates the word's meaning.

mural

Definition: a picture, usually of great size, painted on a wall
Synonym: some possible answers are *panorama, painting, wall illustration*
Illustration: answers will vary

16. Explain how the word relates to the chapter. Answers will vary.

Using Your Inferencing Skills

17. Though they were born in different time periods, Thomas Hart Benton and George Caleb Bingham were both important Missouri artists. Describe the similarities of their work.

Answers will vary. Both artists painted events and people from Missouri's history, from scenes of everyday life to scenes of elections and politics.

18. Why do you think many writers write about things and events that are familiar to them?

Answers will vary. Main point is that writing about familiar things and events makes writing easier and more interesting for both the writer and the reader.

19. Of all the creative Missourians discussed in this chapter, which one do you admire the most? Explain why.

Answers will vary.

20. Choose one of the following activities to complete below:
     • Write a poem about the struggles of being a student.
     • Write a fiction story about a school adventure.
     • Write a paragraph about everyday life in Missouri and draw an illustration based on your paragraph.

Answers will vary. Teachers may adapt the blank scoring guides to score this question.

WEBSITE BIBLIOGRAPHY

Arabia Steamboat Museum: <http://www.1856.com/index.html>

Thomas Hart Benton. Fact Monster: <http://www.factmonster.com/ce6/people/A0807071.html>

Thomas Hart Benton. U-S-History.com: <http://u-s-history.com/pages/h274.html>

George Caleb Bingham. Kansas City Public Library: <http://kclibrary.org/sc/bio/bingham.htm>

George Caleb Bingham. Fact Monster: <http://www.factmonster.com/ce6/people/A0807596.html>

Nathan Boone Homestead State Historic Site. Missouri State Parks and Historic Sites:
    http://www.mostateparks.com/boonehome/photos.htm>

Boone's Lick State Historic Site. Missouri State Parks and Historic Sites:
    <http://www.mostateparks.com/booneslick/geninfo.htm>

George Washington Carver National Monument. National Park Service: <http://www.nps.gov/gwca/expanded/gwc.htm>

The Hermitage, Home of President Andrew Jackson: <http://www.thehermitage.com>

Andrew Jackson. State Library of North Carolina: <http://statelibrary.dcr.state.nc.us/nc/bio/public/jackson.htm>

Thomas Jefferson's First Inaugural Address. Bartleby: <http://www.bartleby.com/124/pres16.html>

Missouri Constitution. Missouri General Assembly: <http://www.moga.state.mo.us/const/moconstn.htm>

Sainte Genevieve, Mo., Historic Homes. <http://www.saintegenevieve.tourism.org/homes.htm>

Taum Sauk Mountain State Park. Missouri State Parks and Historic Sites:
    <http://www.mostateparks.com/taumsauk/geninfo.htm>

ABOUT THE AUTHOR

Pamela Fleming Lowe is a fourth grade eMINTS teacher and MAP Class 10 Leader in Poplar Bluff, Missouri. Her articles have appeared on techLearning.com and she has presented technology and education workshops. She maintains a classroom web site used by educators worldwide: http://schoolweb.missouri.edu/poplarbluff.k12.mo.us/lowe. She was recently voted Teacher of the Year by the Poplar Bluff School District.

Ms. Lowe dedicates this book to her parents, Bob and Ruth Fleming, with thanks for her Missouri history, and to her sister, Robin, for cherished early Missouri memories.